Missions amidst Pagodas: Contextual Communication of the Gospel in the Burmese Buddhist Context

Peter Thein Nyunt

MONOGRAPHS

© 2014 by Peter Thein Nyunt.

Published 2014 by Langham Monographs
an imprint of Langham Creative Projects.

Langham Partnership
PO Box 296, Carlisle, Cumbria CA3 9WZ, UK
www.langham.org

ISBNs:
978-1-78368-984-2 Print
978-1-78368-982-8 Mobi
978-1-78368-983-5 ePub

Peter Thein Nyunt has asserted his right under the Copyright, Designs and Patents Act, 1988 to be identified as the Author of this work.

All rights reserved. No part of this publication may be reproduced, stored in a retrieval system or transmitted, in any form or by any means, electronic, mechanical, photocopying, recording or otherwise, without the prior written permission of the publisher or the Copyright Licensing Agency.

All Scripture quotations, unless otherwise indicated, are from the Holy Bible, New International Version®, NIV®. Copyright © 1973, 1978, 1984, 2011 by Biblica, Inc.™ Used by permission of Zondervan. All rights reserved worldwide. www.zondervan.com The "NIV" and "New International Version" are trademarks registered in the United States Patent and Trademark Office by Biblica, Inc.™

British Library Cataloguing in Publication Data
Nyunt, Peter Thein, author.
Missions amidst pagodas : contextual communication of the Gospel in Burmese Buddhist context
  1. Protestant churches--Missions--Burma--Rangoon.
  2. Christianity and other religions--Buddhism.
  3. Buddhism--Relations--Christianity.
  4. Conversion--Christianity--Case studies.
  5. Rangoon (Burma)—Church history
  I. Title
266'.023'09591-dc23

ISBN-13: 9781783689842

Cover & Book Design: projectluz.com

Langham Partnership actively supports theological dialogue and a scholar's right to publish but does not necessarily endorse the views and opinions set forth, and works referenced within this publication or guarantee its technical and grammatical correctness. Langham Partnership does not accept any responsibility or liability to persons or property as a consequence of the reading, use or interpretation of its published content.

Dr Peter Thein Nyunt holds vital roles in Myanmar as professor, strategist and one of Asia's significant missiologists of the 21st century. He skillfully integrates both theory and practice in his consistent ministry to the Rakhine people within his Buddhist nation. I commend *Missions amidst Pagodas* for its attempt to communicate Christ in indigenous ways within the Burmese Buddhist context. His careful cultural analysis will quicken thinking and stir creative intellectual juices. While some may not fully agree with his using nirvana as equivalent to biblical heaven, his discussions should be read thoughtfully and pondered intently. This is a refreshing and stimulating book.

Dr Alex G. Smith
Buddhist World Advocate, OMF International

This is such an important book—well-researched, cogently argued, clearly expressed. It should be read and studied by everyone who wishes to show the good news of Jesus with Buddhists in Myanmar.

Rev Dr David Harley
Former Principal of All Nations Christian College, UK
former General Director of OMF International

This should be a handbook for Christian organizations, churches and mission practitioners who are being engaged in Christian communication with the Buddhist world.

Rev Dr Mar Gay Gyi
Former President of Myanmar Council of Churches
and Myanmar Baptist Convention

My faithful co-worker, Dr Peter Thein Nyunt, has very rich experience in communicating the good news with our Buddhist brethren. His profound missiological insights in *Missions amidst Pagodas* are incredible. I recommend all disciples of Jesus Christ who have passion to communicate the gospel with the Buddhists should read this book.

Rev Dr Aung Mang
Former Principal of Myanmar Evangelical Graduate School of Theology (MEGST)
and Director of Theological Commission of Myanmar Evangelical Christian Fellowship

Contents

Foreword xi
Preface xiii
Prologue xv
    My Motivation xvii
    Methodology and Terminological Clarification xix

Chapter 1 1
Mission as Communication
    Principles of Contextual Communication 2
    Contextual Conversion 10
    Contextual Congregations 15
    Summary 17

Chapter 2 19
Biblical Perspective of Contextual Communication
    The Bible and Communication 19
    Orality in Communication 22
        Oral Communication in the Old Testament 23
        Oral Communication in Jesus' Ministry 25
        Orality in the Pauline Tradition 28
    Using Oral Tools for Communicating Mission 30
    Summary 33

Chapter 3 35
Socio-Cultural Religious Context of the Burmese in Yangon City
    A Brief History of the Burmese People 35
    Emergence of Nationalism 38
        Buddhism as Nationalism 39
    Social Organization of the Burmese People 41
        Social Classes in Burmese Societies 41
        Burmese Social Values 43
    Historic Influences on the Burmese Worldview 50
    Burmese Religious Values 52
        The Concept of Kamma, Merit and Reincarnation 55
        The Nature of Sin: Kammic Consequences 57
    Summary 59

Chapter 4 61
Missionaries' Communicational Approaches in Yangon City
    Missionaries' Communicational Approaches (1813-1966) 61
        Literature Ministry 62
        Zayat Ministry 63
        Educational Ministry 65
        Medical Ministry 66
    Examining Missionaries' Communicational Approaches 68
        Lack of Credibility of the Communicator Principle 68
        Lack of Frame of Reference Principle 71
        Lack of Contextualization 72
    The National Christian Church (1966 to Present) 74
    Summary 76

Chapter 5 79
Contemporary Christian Communication in Yangon City
    Results of the Interviews 79
        Goals for Communication 82
        Communication Approaches 83
        Communication Methods and Media 84
        Problems and Challenges 86
        The Contributive Factors to accepting the Gospel 87
    Summary and Conclusion 87
    Analysis of the Results from the Survey of Burmese
        Buddhist Converts 89
        Demographic Information 89
        The Communicators and the Media Channels 90
        The Context 92
        The Result from the Understanding of the Gospel 93
    Summary 94

Chapter 6 95
A Paradigm of Contextual Communication
    Communicational Strategies 96
        Family Networks for Communication through
            Family Networks 96
        Patron-Client Communication 98
        Communication through Burmese Religious and
            Cultural Practices 99
    Christological Message 101

  Ecclesiastical Structure 108
    Alternative Models of Contextual Local Congregations 109
    An Ecclesiological Evaluation of the Congregational Models ... 112
    Contextual Evaluation of the Congregational Models 115
  Summary 119

Chapter 7 121
Recommendations and Conclusions
  Recommendations 121
  Recommendations for Further Study 127

Conclusion 129

Bibliography 131

Appendix A 141
Demographic Questionnaire for Interviewees

Appendix B 143
Interview Questions

Appendix C 145
Questionnaire for the Burmese Buddhist Converts in Yangon

Dedicated
to
Rakhine Missions Band for Christ

Dedicated

Foreword

Effective communication of the gospel message in any cultural context is a complex and yet very crucial aspect of the ministry. Christian workers who venture to minister among people other than their own have to be equipped with specific insights, skills and tools for relevant contextual communication. Contextual communication of the gospel being a universal concern, scholars primarily from Europe and North America have attempted to provide specialized insights so as to enable missionaries to serve in the cross cultural context. Apparently, most of what was developed from the Western perspectives had been written with Western assumptions, having limited applicability for the non-western context. Although the "etic" perspective, which the Western scholars have provided in the field of communication has been perceived as a valuable contribution, the urgent need for developing an "emic" or insider's perspective has been evident. Dr Peter Thein Nyunt's *Missions amidst Pagodas: Contextual Communication of the Gospel in the Burmese Buddhist Context* is an attempt that takes into consideration the issue of contextual communication from "emic" or insider's perspective. The author being a Rakhine Buddhist convert himself brings a significant amount of insider's perspectives which are invaluable, but most importantly, being a former Buddhist monk, his perspective provides additional insights for effective contextual communication of the gospel to the Buddhist community in Myanmar.

Dr Peter Thein Nyunt is one of those few Asian scholars with a Buddhist background who have attempted to provide scholarly and contextually relevant ways for communicating the gospel in the Buddhist context. He has meticulously developed a relevant model for contextual communications among the Buddhists by studying communication theories, engaging with contemporary academic literature, taking into consideration the Buddhist background realities and combining his Buddhist background and insights. Further, he takes us through a journey of the Biblical, theoretical, historical and Burmese ways of contextual communication and provides a comprehensive perspective that certainly is helpful for effective communication of the gospel among the Buddhists.

It was my privilege to be Peter's guide during his doctoral studies at South Asia Institute of Advanced Christian Studies, Bangalore. Throughout his time here at SAIACS, Peter passionately pursued his studies with a deep sense of commitment that demonstrated his profound interest and excitement in pursuing his research in the area of contextual communication of the gospel in the Buddhist context. Part of the reason for his excitement was the subject that he was researching was very close to his heart. I found him to be an exciting student who took his research and studies seriously so as to make the gospel communication contextually relevant for his own Buddhist people.

Those who are involved in ministry among the Buddhists will find this book to be informative, insightful, and contextually relevant. Although primarily written for the Burmese Buddhist context, useful insights can be gained by those who are working among the Buddhist people around the world. A timely and relevant contribution in the field of contextual communication in the Buddhist context, I heartily commend this book to the global community of scholars, researchers, mission practitioners as well as those who are interested in working among the Buddhist people.

Atul Y. Aghamkar, PhD
Chairman of Evangelical Fellowship of India
Professor and Head Department of Missiology,
South Asia Institute of Advanced Christian Studies
Bangalore, India, October 5, 2013

Preface

Christian communication is still alien to the Burmese Buddhists even though Protestant Christianity has endeavored to preach the gospel to them for almost two hundred years. Examining Christian communication approaches among these people shows that thousands of missionaries, millions of dollars, and countless translations of texts have been utilized. However, Christianity among these Burmese Buddhists is still regarded as a "potted plant" as it has not been successfully transplanted onto the Burmese soil. This book develops a paradigm of contextual communication of the gospel to these Burmese Buddhists through examining missional approaches of Protestant churches in Yangon city.

Missions amidst Pagodas grew out of my PhD dissertation for South Asia Institute of Advanced Christian Studies (SAIACS), *Toward a Paradigm of Christian Communication for the Bamar Buddhists in Yangon City*. The original dissertation is an academic exercise about the historical and contemporary Christian communicational approaches to the Burmese Buddhists in Yangon and their responses. I have dropped large sections and reworked the text to make it more accessible for a wider readership. I owe a debt of gratitude to many for the part they have played. I pray that this book will help to provoke profound missiological insights for all who have great burden to reach the Buddhists with the gospel in Myanmar and beyond.

Peter Thein Nyunt
Yangon, MYANMAR

Prologue

Myanmar has for centuries been a strong Buddhist country. It is often referred to as the Land of Pagodas because Buddhists have erected pagodas on every hill or mountain near a town or village. According to a well-known Burmese Buddhist monk, Ashin Thittila, in Asian countries the development of the culture of a society is religiously oriented (2000, 213). The social solidarity caused by the integrative religious overlay is strong in Burmese society, and the culture itself is deeply steeped in "Theravada Buddhism." Consequently, the Burmese Buddhist philosophy is all-pervasive, permeating the concepts and worldview of a people and saturating their culture, language, education and attitudes with Buddhistic views. S Ngun Ling states it in this way:

> The Burman culture is deeply embedded in the Theravada form of Buddhist tradition. Theravada Buddhism is the only foundation of the creativity, philosophical thinking and way of life of the overall Burman people. Theravada Buddhist *Abhidharma* philosophy expresses their worldview, their conception of the meaning of human existence, human destiny and also the idea of the Ultimate or God. Religion and culture are, for them, just two sides of a coin (2006, 40).

This interconnectedness of religion and nationality in the socio-cultural identity of the Burmese impedes the penetration of the gospel. That is why Adoniram Judson, the first American Baptist missionary to Myanmar, cried out, "It was easier to extract a tooth from the tiger's mouth than to convert a Burmese Buddhist to Christian faith" (Clasper 1968, 16). Nowadays, the population of Myanmar is estimated at 60 million, and Christianity stands at 9.1% (including non-Burmese ethnic groups), whereas about 0.1% of Burmese put their trust in Christian beliefs (Nyunt 2008, 104). Despite the fact that Protestant Christianity has been in Myanmar for two hundred years, Christian communication to the Burmese Buddhists is still confronted by failure to make a significant impact. This failure of communication involves both Burmese Buddhists' barriers and Christian missiological weaknesses.

In addressing the problems confronting Christian communication, one of the remarkable factors out of many, is that Christianity in Myanmar is still alienated in the Burmese Buddhist society. Circumstances led them to be suspicious of Christianity as an alien religion or the religion of Westerners. To depict this chronic problem, S Pau Kham En states that Christian communications to the Burmese Buddhists are suspected as "part of the western invasion of their cultural and spiritual realm" (2003, 19). This suspicion has been perpetuated until today so that Christians are envisaged as a detrimental menace, which may hamper the nationalism and solidarity of the country in many ways. In fact, there is nothing intrinsically wrong with the gospel, but Christian communication and churches are erroneously seen as outside intrusions, and foreign imports to be avoided like the plague. In addition, the case is worse when the majority of Christians comprise various minority ethnic groups in Myanmar who are suspected by the non-Christians as being pro-Westerners.

From the Christian point of view, there are also apparent missiological weaknesses in mission strategy, ineffective Christian communication, and lack of indigeneity in particular. In regard to mission strategy, the churches in Myanmar still venerate the imported mission outreach or strategy inherited for centuries without critical appraisal of their relevance. Under the colonial period, the "mission station approach" was common. In its time, it may have been the only viable way to help Christians survive and to get the church started. But the "gathered conglomerate," often separates converts from their people and society and makes less impact on the core of Buddhist people groups. In addition, due to the tactless approaches of some Christian fanatics to convert people to Christianity, Christian communication has failed largely in most of the fertile grounds of Burmese soil.

Looking at the church in Myanmar, it is usually seen as an alien form and a foreign institution of the West. Frequently, the church looks like an imported monstrosity. Its buildings, forms, music, and behaviors are often so different from those of the Burmese Buddhist society. While of necessity there will be differences, too often the church sticks out like a sore thumb or a nail that must be pounded down. This lack of indigeneity makes Christian communication ineffective, particularly among the Burmese Buddhists.

My Motivation

I was brought up in a staunch Rakhine Buddhist family on an island in the Rakhine State, the western part of Myanmar. Significantly, all inhabitants on that island are Buddhists devoted to Theravada Buddhism. Being an islander and influenced by Buddhism, I had a strong determination to be a Buddhist monk. Accordingly, after my high school graduation I came to Yangon for the purpose of studying Buddhist scriptures, and at the age of 20 was ordained as a monk. Then I began to study Buddhist scriptures thoroughly. During my monkhood, one day while pondering the ethical disciplines (227 precepts) that every Buddhist monk has to observe, I asked myself if my good works and following these precepts could save me. Then, I began to worry about my future life after death as I realized that neither observing those disciplines nor my good works and religion could save me. I was moved to seek the solution for the assurance of salvation.

After a couple of weeks I met a Christian pastor near our monastery and discussed with him the way for salvation in Jesus Christ. In fact, I used to look at Christianity from a negative perspective for a variety of reasons. But a fresh wind of the Holy Spirit touched my heart and I realized that I was a sinner in need of forgiveness of sins through Jesus Christ. Six months later, in November 1990, I accepted him as my personal Savior and served him as Lord. From then onward, I had a burning desire to share the gospel with Buddhists. After finishing a B.A in Theology from Evangel Bible College in 1995, I started a small church within the Burmese Buddhist community in Yangon. I soon noted that a few Burmese people, often young people, who became Christians, all faced intense pressure from their Buddhist family and neighbors, which led to their expulsion from their family. At the same time, these Burmese converts found it difficult to be satisfactorily integrated into the Christian community. Most likely it was due to these hardships that some of the first converts returned to the Buddhist faith of their Burmese community. As a pastor, I have had to struggle with this problem, which is well known by all missions working among Buddhists. Experiences like these and realities in mission works within the Burmese community as mentioned led me to ask why the gospel is still alien to the Burmese and its impact is still regarded as a 'potted plant' in the Burmese soil. Taking serious consideration of these issues ignited me to attempt this study.

This book is based on my PhD research of the Burmese Buddhists in Yangon and written in anticipation that it will hold significance for the following reasons. The original study was delimited only for the Burmese Buddhists in Yangon city, and is not a comparative study of Buddhism and Christianity, nor an in-depth study of Buddhism. However, this book will point to solutions to some of the problems the churches have struggled with in trying to communicate the gospel with Burmese Buddhists. Through this book, I expect that guidelines will emerge for increasing the effectiveness of mission projects of churches and for setting up new Burmese mission projects in other parts of the country as well. I also expect that all Bible school and/or seminary-trained Myanmar Christian workers, as well as informally trained lay leaders and their counterparts from all other regions of Myanmar, will have great concern for the Buddhists in the country. In addition, it is expected that this study will contribute to the development of missiological insights concerning mission to Burmese Buddhists. Together with similar studies being carried out among other Theravadic Buddhists in Asia and beyond, this book will hopefully contribute to the churches some principles and guidelines in developing a paradigm of contextual communication of the gospel to the Buddhists. Last, but not least, this book will be significant for expatriate mission workers planning to serve or presently serving the Lord in Myanmar.

Methodology and Terminological Clarification

The multiple nature of the missiological topic under consideration requires a multidisciplinary approach in researching it. In this study of Christian communication with the Burmese Buddhists, many fields of study were investigated including the socio-cultural religious context of the Burmese people, survey and interview methodologies, biblical and theological perspectives of Christian communication, communication theory, anthropology, and missiology. In multiple ways these fields and topics are interwoven and nearly inseparable. Although each of these disciplines may contribute from various angles and in various degrees, the fields of study that may contribute most significantly toward building a theoretical foundation to the topic were communication theory, anthropological and missiological approaches.

Historically and originally, the term Burmese has been used as a label for the majority ethnic group. This group constitutes approximately 70% of the total population of the whole country. Various authors in literature have termed this group as "Burman, Burmah, Bahma, Bamar or Burmese. Even in my original dissertation I used the term "Bamar." But this book aims for a wider readership, so I shall use the term "Burmese" for the majority group and official language, and Myanmar for representing the country and all its citizens.

CHAPTER 1

Mission as Communication

Mission is at the very heart of the gospel and the life of church. God's actions in mission are manifested in the context in which people live and of course his mission always takes place in a specific social context (Hesselgrave 1978, 21). David J. Bosch believes that to summarize God's actions in mission, "one of the best words available to us is the word communication" (1993, 188). Mission cannot be understood without communication as an indispensable part of God's mission. Hence, if the church is on the move and its mission is to be effective, work in the arena of communication is essential.

Mission is not a by-product of ecclesiology or of soteriology. It originates and anchors itself in our communicating God. It is spelled out as the participation of the church in the *missio Dei* to communicate his work in reconciling sinful humankind to himself. The *missio Dei* takes shape in innumerable specific places and times (Bosch 1992, 13). In this regard, it is related to the concept of missions. F Hrangkhuma states that in a narrower and more specific sense, the plural 'missions' is often more appropriate than the singular (1995, 183). It underscores the church's specific and deliberate activities to communicate the reality of God and his salvation to achieve the goals among a particular group of people, but the purpose of *missio Dei* should remain the same.

Evangelism is integral to mission and takes place only when there is communication. John Stott agrees that the primary importance within God's mission is evangelism which is sufficiently distinct and yet not separate from mission (1975, 113). Bosch also states:

> Mission includes *evangelism* as one of its essential dimensions. Evangelism is the proclamation of salvation in Christ to those who do not believe in him, calling them to repentance and conversion, announcing forgiveness of sin and inviting them to become living members of Christ's earthly community and to begin a life of service to others in the power of the Holy Spirit (1992, 10-11).

Following Bosch, I define evangelism as communication of the gospel in *missio Dei*, and in consequence, it must always be contextual. In this study, mission among the Burmese Buddhists in Yangon has consisted of more than evangelism alone; it has included social services for the betterment of the life of the Burmese. In my evaluation of the communication of the gospel to the Burmese, however, I will look at the impact of this communication only in terms of conversion and incorporation into local congregations.

Principles of Contextual Communication

Communication is the lifeblood of society. It is vital to the functioning of human social order and constructive of culture. No culture can breathe without communication. An understanding of Burmese culture will serve to widen the field of communication and extend its discursive boundaries. It will also help communication research to be contextualized more productively. In this sense, communication of the gospel is similar to all other forms of communication, which have a message that a communicator wants to communicate to a receptor. Therefore, we may learn from some sound principles of communication theory for our communication of the gospel. Thus, for the purpose of this study I develop eleven principles of contextual communication. In that process a model of communication is to be used to analyze the work of selected churches of Christian communication to the Burmese Buddhists in Yangon context.

Contextual communication takes place when the communicator has a clear purpose and goals for the message. Therefore, the purpose of communication is to create the intended understanding of the content of the message that substantially corresponds with the intent of the communicator. This in turn leads the receptor to discover that the message meets his or her felt-needs and to respond to it accordingly. As Smith says, "The legitimate purpose of communication is to gain access to the mind through the gate of understanding" (1992, 21). From a Christian perspective, the goals may be considered statements of faith that delineate what we believe God wants to bring about through our communication of the gospel. The purpose of evangelism is to communicate the gospel so that people may understand it and respond through conversion and incorporation into local congregations

Contextual communication is a personal interaction between the communicator and the receptor. Smith quotes Augsburger as saying, "communication is co-response-ability" (Ibid., 25). His emphasis is that communication takes place only when there is involvement. This participatory approach presupposes a mutual relationship in which the communicators not only endeavor to make themselves and their message understood by the receptors, but also strive to understand the receptor and his or her response as well (Ibid., 27-29). Charles H Kraft has pointed to the personal nature of God's communicational strategy, which should characterize all Christian communication. "Incarnation-personal participation in the lives of his receptors is his constant method. And as in all life-changing communication, the person (whether God himself in Christ or another person as God's representative) is a major component of the message conveyed" (1991, 17). Thus, the personal nature of Christian communication has to do with the relational nature of the message. Just as God wants to establish a relationship with human beings through his communication, Christian gospel communicators want to include the receptors in their fellowship with God and with one another in the church. Therefore, "communicators who seek to present a message recommending a relationship must model the relationship they recommend if their message is to be effective. Thus, Christian communicators are a more essential part of the message they communicate than a communicator of non-relational kinds of information" (Ibid., 18).

Contextual communication presupposes a thorough knowledge of the receptor by the communicator. In the communication process the role of the receptor is as crucial as that of the communicators. "Receptors are active, even when they seem to be just sitting there. They are not simply passive recipients of whatever is sent their way. They interact in a transactional process in which the results are negotiated on the spot rather than predetermined" (Ibid., 67). When the communicators have encoded their message and it reaches the receptors through the channel selected by the communicators, the receptors start decoding the message. This is a selective filtering process which includes four stages: exposure, attention, comprehension, and retention. It is the receptors who give meaning to the message and, based on their understanding of it and its relevance to their situation, then respond to questions such as, "Who are the receptors? Where are they? What are their needs?" This will then help the communicators to give their message a format and to select the appropriate media that are appropriate for the situation of the receptors (Sogaard 1993, 99).

The selection of channels for the communication of the message is crucial for the receptor's perception. No human communication is possible except through the use of verbal or non-verbal signal systems used in face-to-face communication in media (Smith 1992, 19). In order to communicate a message effectively, the communicator also needs to know the culture of the receptor because of the variety in communication channels from one culture to another. The communicator should select and shape the channels according to the receptor's context, experiences, and preferences (Ibid., 19). Furthermore, the communicator should be aware of which para-messages certain signal systems and media may convey along with the main message. Such unintended para-messages may overshadow the main message and influence the receptor's understanding and response in a negative way. For example, communicating the gospel through literacy-based media in a predominantly non-literate society may convey the message that Christianity is a religion only for those who have learned to read and write.

Contextual communication requires that the receptor should have a high regard for the communicator if contextual communication is to take place (Dodd 1982, 10-11, see also Kraft 1991, 150, 156-159). The message is not only to be spoken and heard but also to be seen in the communicator himself. This means that effective communication of the message comes not only from the lips but it is embodied in the communicator. In other words, the message cannot be divorced from the communicator. This is in line with the Burmese saying, *"pauk-ko-khin- hma- taya-myin,"* meaning that if the relationship is built between receptor and the communicator, and especially when the receptor trusts the communicator, his message earns credibility from the receptor.

For contextual communication to take place, the message should be communicated in all the three dimensions. Hiebert says:

> Taken together, cognitive, affective, and evaluative assumptions provide people with a way of looking at the world that makes sense out of it, that gives them a feeling of being at home, and that reassures them that they are right. This world view serves as the foundation on which they construct their explicit belief and value systems, and the social institutions within which they live their daily lives (1985, 47-48).

On the cognitive level, the gospel communication has to do with knowledge and truth. But passing on information is not enough. It must touch the affective dimensions through joy, comfort and the like. A feeling of affection and loyalty is important. But communicating the gospel also has to do with values and allegiances. It is at the evaluative level that each culture judges value and determines right and wrong.

Culture is the only vehicle of communication known to human beings. That is why God entered into Hebraic and Grecian cultures to communicate his message of love. The incarnation of Jesus is the classic example of entering into the receptor's culture for effective communication. Imposition from outside, using alien cultural symbols and channels of communication can never be effective.

Contextual communication is not just an event but a process or a series of events. Seen from the perspective of the communicator, it is "a consecutive, interrelated number of communication processes, some of short-term duration, others involving years, which are going on at the same time" (Sogaard 1993, 30-31). Seen from the perspective of the receptor, communication takes place as a process over time within a specific context, and of course, the receptor moves through the various stages of his or her life. Sogaard has pointed out:

> Our communication messages must be designed as a process that corresponds to the needs of a receptor at his or her present position or stage in life and the needs and problems faced at that time. A person's relationship with God can be seen as a spiritual journey and if we know a person's position in this journey, we can design communication events that will be relevant at this time (Ibid., 31).

Contextual communication is receptor-oriented. In order for the receptor to understand the message of the communicator accurately, the communicator and the receptor have to operate within the same "frame of reference" (Kraft 1991, 23). Communicators, therefore, must choose whether their communication will take place within their own frame of reference or within the frame of reference of the receptor. In contextual communication, the communicator is the one to make adjustments to the context of the receptor by adopting the latter's frame of reference. If the gospel is not communicated within the frame of reference which Kraft calls the identification approach, the alternative may be an extractionist approach, which at times projects the gospel as foreign to the culture and excludes those who respond to it from their culture (Kraft 1979, 147-155).

Contextual communication seeks to express the relevance of the gospel in the context of receptors while at the same time being faithful to the text of the gospel. It presupposes that the communicator needs to find new ways of communicating the gospel to perceive its relevance and appropriateness to the receiving community in each specific context (Taber 1978, 7). My understanding of the biblical text follows the model developed by Kraft called "the Bible as inspired classic casebook."

> The Bible, then, is seen as an inspired collection of classic cases from history . . . exemplifying certain of God's past interactions with human beings for the instruction and guidance of

> those who seek to follow in their footsteps . . . This model simply speaks to the fact that the Scriptures are a collection of 'classic' materials (i.e. time-tested and found to be of enduring value) that were produced for particular people at particular times and places. When there is in the Bible historical and theological systematization, it is done with particular target audience and situation in mind. Each document is a specific presentation dealing with the problems and participants in a specific context (1979, 398).

In accordance with this way of understanding the Bible, human beings today, each in their own context, are called to have dynamic interactions with God similar to those between God and the Biblical persons (Ibid., 207). Since we do not have one pure culture-free gospel, but a gospel inculturated by a variety of cultures, we would not be faithful to the text if we simply copied the theology and church structures from the first century congregations in Greece, or imposed a Western understanding of the text on people in another culture. Faithfulness to the text lies in encouraging people today in the midst of their context to have interactions with God that lead to faithful allegiance to God like those we find in the biblical text (Gilliland 1989, 12).

In the words of Charles R Taber, to communicate the gospel in a way that is relevant in the context involves an "effort to understand and take seriously the specific context of each human group and person on its own terms and in all its dimensions—cultural, religious, social, political, economic—and to discern what the gospel says to people in that context" (1979, 146). Taber elaborates on what it means to relate the gospel to specific contexts as follows:

> What usable concepts and symbols does this religion provide for the approach of the gospel, on the analogy of Paul's use of the Athenian "unknown god"? What genuine insights does it offer into the character, activity and will of God? What are its gaps, its errors, its distortions? What particular obstacles does it place in the way of a true understanding of the gospel? It is

on the basis of such an analysis that contextualization tries to discover in the Scriptures what God is saying to these people. In other words, contextualization takes very seriously the example of Jesus in the sensitive and careful way he offered each person a gospel tailored to his or her own context (Ibid., 146).

Contextual communication, which requires faithfulness to the text and relevance to the context, follows the dynamic equivalence model, developed by Kraft on the basis of translation theories. These translation theories maintain that:

> The aim of translation is to bring about equivalence between the response of the contemporary hearers/readers of the translation and that of the original hearers/readers of the communication recorded in the document being translated. This model sees the translated Word acting as a communicational stimulus toward the re-creation of an impact on today's receptors that is (roughly) equivalent to that recorded in the Word (1979, 402).

Just as a text is translated from one language to another, so the Christian faith in word and life has to be transculturated from one culture to another. The purpose of this transculturation is to "represent the meanings of the historical events as if they were clothed in contemporary events" (Ibid., 280). Through such a "re-creation of equivalent events in today's cultural contexts" (Ibid., 281), the same responses of commitment to God as those of biblical persons can be elicited from contemporary people in their specific context. This model of dynamic equivalence may be applied not only to communication of the gospel but also to theologizing, to the development of church structures, worship forms, and all other aspects of the Christian life and ministry.

Much more can be said about the theory of contextual communication. The eleven principles introduced here are to be applied in a specific situation, using relevant techniques and methods of communication appropriately in the particular context of Burmese Buddhists in Yangon.

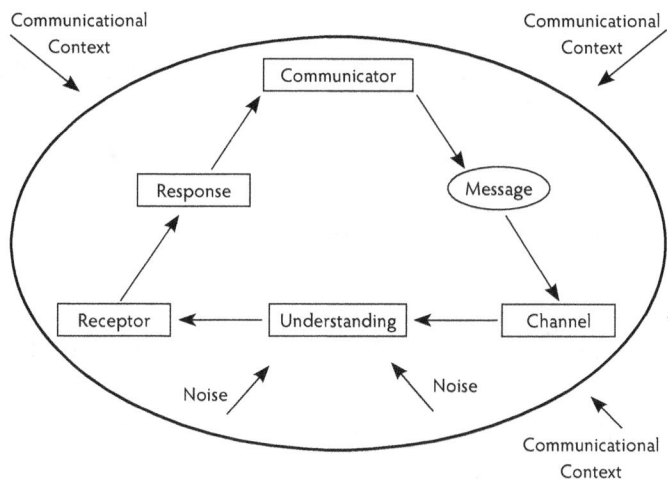

FIGURE 1: A Model for Analysis of the Communication of the Gospel

For the purpose of this study, the simplified model of communication (above) has been developed to reflect the basic principles described in the previous section and to identify the elements used in this analysis. Within this simplified model (Figure 1), the triangular flow highlights the three basic elements in any communication process: the communicator, the channel, and the receptor. Communication is an interaction through a channel between the communicator and the receptor. The meaning of the message in the mind of the communicator is not necessarily identical to the one in the mind of the receptor. Similarly, the response of the receptor to the message is not necessarily identical to the intended effect that the communicator had in mind. Finally, the model illustrates that communication takes place within a context, which influences all aspects of the communication process.

This model is to be used to present an overview of the communicational interaction of Burmese Buddhists with the gospel and the Protestant churches in Yangon. The communicational situation with the Burmese Buddhists in Yangon may be summarized like this: the Protestant churches in Yangon are the communicators (C) who encode the message (M) of the gospel, and the receptors (R) the Burmese Buddhists are the audience.

Based on their understanding of the Burmese receptors and the Yangon context, the communicators encode the gospel in messages and select media or other channels to transmit the messages to the Burmese Buddhists. On the basis of their understanding, some Burmese Buddhists respond by converting to Christ and by becoming members of local congregations. The contexts of the Burmese Buddhists and the context of the church influence all aspects of the communication process.

This model will later be used to analyze the basic elements in the communication of the gospel to the Burmese Buddhists. The elements of the communication process will be described, and an attempt will be made to explain the process. Finally, the model will be used to identify critical issues for the effective communication of the gospel for the Burmese Buddhists in Yangon city, Myanmar.

Contextual Conversion

The goal of communicating the gospel is conversion. The word conversion has a broad connotation; however, as a basis it means "a change of direction with a total reorientation of outlook and objectives" (Pentecost 1982, 117). It begins in the mind and is demonstrated in attitudes and actions. It involves response and change concerning views and behavior. The basic meaning of the key words for conversion in both the Old Testament (Hebrew: *shuv*) and the New Testament (Greek: *epistrepho*) is turning or returning (Ibid.,117). Conversion is a "turning, in the sense of changing or reversing the direction, in which one is headed so that it is toward rather than away from God, and this turning is accompanied with the need for repentance, *metanoia* in Greek (Kraft 1979, 333). This reorientation comes in response to a call or invitation from God, and involves a turning away from something or someone that is renounced, and a turning to something or someone that is embraced. The Bible gives many cases of conversion, but it never presents a single prescribed form. Mainly, biblical principles of conversion take place through reorientation, expression, personal decision, incorporation, worldview and behavioral changes.

A contextual conversion takes place within the culture. A scriptural example of this is found in the book of Acts before the Jerusalem council (Acts 15). Up until that time the early church commonly required Gentiles to "convert" to the Jewish culture/religion as a prerequisite for their conversion to Christ. In fact, changing culture/religion is not a prerequisite for, nor a guarantee of, salvation; conversion is a matter of the heart (Lim 2010, 33). That is why a contextual conversion, such as that which the Jerusalem council agreed upon at the recommendations of Paul and Peter, involves the convert being allowed and encouraged to express his or her new faith within his or her own culture. Hans Kasdorf states:

> The meeting point is that of reconciliation, the point when the person – regardless of his religious or cultural status – becomes a new person in Christ. This does not mean that he becomes *neos*, or new in point of time, but *kairos*, or new in point of quality. Thus when a person is converted to God, it does not mean that Christ Jesus makes all Jews into Gentiles or all Gentiles into Jews; He produces a new kind of person out of both, although they remain Gentiles and Jews (1980, 87).

This shows that contextual conversion takes place with reference to points of contact already present in the culture of the convert. God has already provided points of contact for the gospel within every culture, and he uses these points of contact when leading people to conversion. This means that elements of God's truth may be found in religions outside of Christianity. As a result, new followers of Jesus do not need to abandon those truth elements to become Christians. For conversion, the key emphasis here is relationship with Jesus himself.

A contextual conversion keeps the convert within his or her sociological group. In a contextual conversion, even the conversion of an individual, the church must always have in mind the larger sociological group to which the convert belongs. Donald McGavran explains the principle of conversion within the sociological group of the convert by pointing out that converts should,

> Remain thoroughly one with their own people in most matters. They should continue to eat what their people eat. They should not say, my people are vegetarians, but now that I have become a Christian I'm going to eat meat. After they become Christians they should be more rigidly vegetarian than they were before. In the matter of clothing, they should continue to look precisely like their kinsfolk. In the matter of marriage, most peoples are endogamous; they insist that, "our people marry only our people". (1992, d-103)

As Jesus promised in Mark 8:34-37, conversion may involve exclusion and persecution from the convert's family and community. Even so, converts should be encouraged and helped to remain with their own people so that on all occasions they will have time to witness to the family of Christ who is in their hearts.

A contextual conversion involves an encounter between the convert's old religion and worldview and his or her new faith in Jesus Christ. Kraft has pointed to three critical encounters between the old and new worldview.

> An allegiance or commitment encounter, leading to a new relationship with God, where allegiance to God takes precedence over all other loyalties . . . A truth encounter, leading to a right understanding about God and the relationship between God and humanity and between humans, in accordance with the biblical teaching . . . A power encounter, where the trust in God replaces the reliance on and/or the fear of other powers, leading to spiritual freedom. (1991, 258-265)

These encounters, which lead to radical changes at the deep worldview level, are reflected in the behavior of the convert. Some aspects of the convert's life will therefore be changed whereas others are incorporated into the new life (Myanmar Council of Churches 2002, 181-184).

In a contextual conversion, the gospel is communicated to the convert according to the indigenous communication patterns within the convert's frame of reference. In "God's inspired casebook" we see how God communicated with people using communication patterns and methods with which the people were already familiar. God still communicates with people in this way. Missionaries working for a contextualized conversion should seek to recognize God's contextual communication with the people, endeavor to use their frame of reference, and work toward discovering the communication channels appropriate to the people's context.

A contextual conversion means that the felt-needs of the receptors are met by the gospel. Although all people irrespective of their culture suffer from the effects of the same fall, the effects take on different forms, creating different needs in each culture and individuals; still all of these needs may be met by the gospel.

A contextual conversion takes place in accordance with the decision-making patterns in the culture of the convert. Conversion to Christ involves a decision but decision-making models vary from culture to culture. Kraft therefore advises that Christian conversion should be in accord with the decision-making patterns of the convert's culture. The advocates of the gospel need to become familiar with those patterns and work within them rather than imposing on the converts the models of their own culture as if their own culture's models alone were Christian (Kraft 1978, 344). For the purposes of this study, I have chosen an adaptation of the conversion model developed by Alan R. Tippett using Van Gennep's theory of rites of passage and his own study of conversion in the Pacific Islands (Tippett 1977, 207). This is a simplified model that is useful in analyzing the spiritual journey of Burmese people.

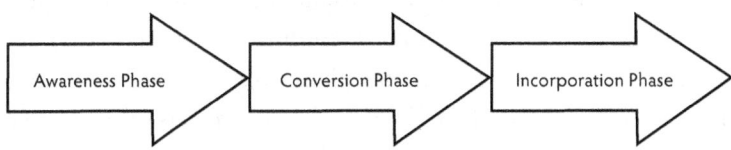

FIGURE 2: Decision-Making Process (Adapted from Tippett 1977, 207)

This model (Figure 2) underscores the idea that the communication of the gospel is not a single event, but a series of communicational events that form a process or a spiritual journey. The conversion process is here depicted as consisting of three phases: awareness, conversion, and incorporation. These three phases might also be considered as three dimensions of the conversion process: the dimension of awareness, the dimension of conversion, and the dimension of incorporation. Whereas Tippett in his original model has a fourth phase, maturation, I follow Seppo Syrjanen, who in his research of the conversion of Muslims in Pakistan combines this phase with the phase of incorporation (Syrjanen 1987, 63-66).

The movement from the awareness phase to the conversion phase is not marked by any observable events; and often the two phases overlap. The awareness of the gospel, that is the understanding of Christianity as an alternative to one's present way of life, may come to individuals or groups by way of discovery through a natural development, through pressure from without, through the internal pressure of a crisis situation, or through direct advocacy. When receptors have not only been exposed to the gospel message, but have also understood it so well that they are ready to respond to it meaningfully, either positively or negatively, they have entered the conversion phase.

In the conversion phase, receptors begin to consider the gospel and its implication for them and finally make a conscious decision to become a follower of Jesus Christ and a member of the church. I consider the initiation rite of baptism, which confirms the converts' change of religious faith and their transfer to the religious community of the church, to be the point of transition between the conversion and the incorporation phase.

When communicating the gospel, it is important to know where the receptors are in their spiritual journey. When the receptors understand the gospel, their relationships to God, to church, and to their original religion and religious community differ according to the phase they are in—the awareness phase, the conversion phase, or the incorporation phase. Depending on the phase, their needs and problems also differ. Therefore, the content and form of the message and the media used to communicate the message must be adapted accordingly.

Contextual Congregations

People are often more impressed with statistics on conversions than with those on making disciples. After a person is converted, they begin the long but essential process of discipleship or Christian nurture. The next step following contextual conversion is to nurture the converts in such a way that they can be made disciples in their own cultural context. For this to happen, the new converts have to be incorporated into a congregation in order to grow and mature in a contextual way. Without forsaking their own cultures, converts need to feel at home and be equipped to cultivate reproductive fellowships through the Word of God. Arn paraphrases the reproductive nature of the Great Commission this way:

> The words of Christ in Matthew 28:19-20 communicate vividly Christ's understanding of a disciple. He saw a disciple as one who becomes a follower, who is taught, who is nurtured in the faith, who in turn goes out to make disciples, who are then taught and nurtured in the faith, who then in turn go out. (1982, 20)

It is a process of equipping converts to grow to maturity and to lead people to become recruiters or leaders. Jesus and Paul in the New Testament were interested primarily in developing these kinds of leaders. According to social science, "leadership is frequently defined as the process of influence" and in making disciples this sort of influence is most effective if disciples are made "within the immediate situation and in the overall community in which they live" (Van Rheenen 1996, 165; see also Wilson 1978, 60-61). There are four specific characteristics of contextual congregations appropriate in the Burmese Buddhist context.

First of all, a contextual-local congregation should aim at helping its members to remain within their own culture and community, so that the congregation is not seen as a foreign element in the context. Instead of extracting its members from their culture and community, the contextual congregation should advocate a contextual conversion (McGavran 1955, 10-11). This congregation should be a fellowship of followers of Jesus who strive to continue to live in fellowship with their non-Christian relatives and neighbors. In attempting to be relevant in its context, a local congregation should never lose its unique Christian identity, which sets the church apart from any other institution. Being faithful to the biblical principles of the church, it will differ from its surroundings in the whole ethos of the Christian fellowship; however, it will never cease to be relevant for the surrounding community because it expresses its message, fellowship, and service in forms and structures that are familiar to the context and it addresses needs that are felt in the community.

Secondly, a contextual congregation should endeavor to use the language of the converts and communication methods with which they are most familiar in services and other activities. One of the most important parts of the context is the language because much of a society's culture is stored in and transmitted through its language. Only when the Word of God is communicated in the mother tongue of the members, and only when the members communicate with one another and with God through their own language, can a congregation be said to be contextual. Moreover, a contextual congregation should attempt to develop and use rituals, symbols, and worship styles which, while communicating the relevant biblical message effectively, address the needs of the members. For literate and non-literate peoples alike, rituals are important for the life of the congregation, "for rituals, like sacred symbols, are languages for speaking of spiritual things (Hiebert 1994, 167). Hiebert asserts that rituals are important to teach new Christians the meaning of the gospel in their new lives and to proclaim the gospel to non-Christians who gather to see what the Christians are doing (1997, 84-86).

Disciples are made in small (not big) groups where a person looks to another person for instruction, counsel, training, and fellowship (Jenson and Stevens 1981, 158). Jesus unfolded his teaching of truth in a relational context—discipleship. He chose twelve people to teach by example in the context of the day-in day-out activities of living together and ministering to people in love and power. A contextual congregation insures that its method of education strengthens each member's faith as well as a sense of belonging to the local and universal church without alienating any from his or her original community or its values. This sort of approach to formal and informal education in the local congregation involves teaching the knowledge of God and skills that are relevant to the members' actual Christian life in the congregation and to their social service and mission in their original community. If the teaching is not done contextually, the content and form of education may alienate the members from their own people within their own context and will not be relevant to the values of their culture (Hiebert 1997, 84-86).

Last but not least, a contextual congregation should seek to employ indigenous organizational structures and leadership forms. Only when the patterns and styles used to govern the life of the fellowship are in harmony with those of the local culture may we speak of a contextual organization and leadership of the local congregation (Smalley 1992, C. 152-154). Moreover, the theology and ethics of the contextual local congregation should be developed by the members of the local congregations as the congregations reflect on their life in their context in light of Scripture. Instead of taking a theology of a dominant Christian group developed in another context, contextual congregations will begin to develop their own understanding of the Christian faith and its implications for them.

Summary

In this chapter, I presented mission as communication that is contextual, and I developed eleven principles of contextual communication. Then to reflect those principles I developed the operational model for communicating the gospel to the Burmese Buddhists in Yangon context. Then, I stated my theological convictions concerning the key issues in the communication of the gospel, namely conversion to Christ and the church of Christ into which converts are incorporated. Following this, the expected outcome of a contextual communication of the gospel, namely contextual conversions and contextual congregations with significant characteristics, was outlined. It involves the entire transference process of making God known in particular contexts. This entire process is impacted by knowing God, which in turn is informed by all of the relevant contextual data. The universal gospel is to be communicated contextually as it is most fundamentally a matter of knowing God within the limitations of culturally specific human contexts. Communication has a number of dimensions; however, it is essential to understand the grounds on which contextual Christian communication rests, and they will be examined only from the biblical perspective in chapter 2.

CHAPTER 2

Biblical Perspective of Contextual Communication

In chapter 1, I established a theoretical framework by revealing that Christian communication is indispensible from mission with its goal of contextual conversion and contextual congregations. Communication as mission is a dynamic process of making God known in particular context (Shaw and Van Engen 2003, xiv). As stated, communication takes place in specific places and times and its content, validity, and meaning are derived from Scripture (Van Engen 1996, 37). It can be stated that without a biblical foundation Christian communication would be inconceivable. A D Manuel states that the Bible is the story of the communication of God with humankind and people's communication with others (1994, 20). Manuel's statement points out that the centrality of the Bible is concerned with communication and this centrality is a written record of communication between God and his chosen people in which God makes himself known to them and they respond to him. The exploration of a biblical perspective of communication provides an essential standard for judging the communication and missiological hermeneutic approaches to the gospel in general and in particular to the Burmese Buddhists in Yangon.

The Bible and Communication

The whole Bible shows God's methods of communication. It is the record of God's self-communication to humankind and their responses to his initiatives. Thus, communication has been central to God as he values relationship. Sundersingh claims that, "one of the central themes of the Bible is to describe the purpose of God's communication" (2001, 42). The word "communication" is conspicuous by its absence in the Bible. Yet the Bible is a communication book looking at the words "God speaks." In this regard, Alex G. Smith states:

> Significantly, in the Bible God "spoke" more than "wrote." . . . In creation God repeatedly "said" and it was done (Gen 1:3f). Throughout Genesis God spoke to Adam and Eve (3:9f); to Cain (4:6-10); to Noah (6:13); to Abram (12:1); to Abimelech (20:3); to Rebekah (25:23); to Isaac (26:2); to Jacob (31:3), and so forth. God spoke directly to Moses (Exod 3:4f); Joshua (Josh 3:7); Gideon (Judg 6:14); Samuel (1 Sam 3:11); David (1 Sam 23:2); Solomon (1 Kings 3:11) and many others. God spoke to the prophets and through them as mouths to the nations. John the Baptist, Jesus and the disciples spoke to individuals, families, and multitudes . . . The Bible is replete with multiple accounts of dialogues between God and men, and amongst humankind themselves (2008,13).

The connotation of these words "God speaks" can be found in the expression "Thus says the Lord . . ." which appears 4000+ times in the Bible, and it has become "the equivalent of God's self-communication in history" (Palakeel 2007, 17). The first communication mentioned in the Bible can be found in Genesis 1:3 where "God said, "Let there be light" and the last communication occurs in the second to last verse, Revelation 22:20, where Jesus is reported as saying, "Yes, I am coming soon." His spoken words to mankind have been kept alive till now through the testimony of the Scriptures. This address of God is taking place by a special intervention of God in human history. In such intervention, "God speaks", means both the act and content of God's self-communication. Thus, the centrality of the Bible is seen as God speaking to all peoples and nations in all possible languages, cultures and media, as a variety of media is the hallmark of his communication.

This formal self-communication of God began with the first man, and continued unabated in spite of the sin of mankind. In short, throughout the Bible and throughout history God has shown himself in variety of ways. Lucien Legrand expresses it this way:

> The God of the Bible is a God who speaks. He speaks to the Patriarchs, sending Abraham on his foundational journey to the land beyond (Gen12:1-3), accompanying him and his descendants with his blessings and promises (13:14-17; 15:1-21; 28:13-15), challenges (22:2, 15-18; 18:10-15, 16-32). He reveals himself to Moses and calls him (Exod 3:4-14). Through his word, he leads his people into freedom . . . God will continue to speak through the prophets whose essential identity is to be God's mouth pieces. Their basic utterance is the "pronouncement formula." Thus says the Lord Yahweh . . . (2003, 9-10).

God not only speaks to human beings but also demonstrates his message through his actions, because words are accompanied with actions in which God reveals himself. Therefore, the communicating God is not just a monologue speaker who bombards us with his one-way speech/commandment; his speech is addressed to human beings and expects a response.

As stated, the Bible is the only record of God and humankind but it is written in a particular context under the inspiration of the Holy Spirit (2 Tim 3:16-17; 2 Pet 1:19-21; 3:15-16). Charles H Kraft describes the Bible as written medium of communication "in terms of the perceptual categories of the cultural frame of reference" of the communicational context (2001, 31). Kraft's elucidation is apt as the Bible is recorded in the human cultural context in which the message of communication has been given. Thus, communication is contextual and in the Old Testament the record of God's communication to Jewish people can be seen in terms of Jewish thought patterns which give rise to typically Jewish responses to his message in the Hebrew language and culture. Likewise, in the New Testament the records of communicational events were written in terms of Greek and Aramaic and Greco-Roman culture (Ibid., 33). These facts show that God initiates his communication where his recipients are, by revealing new insights in a manner comprehensible to them. Then, the receptors have the opportunity to respond to him in faith expressed in appropriate ways in their cultural context. The Bible is the self-communication of God, using all forms and channels of human communication. It is a unique source of experiencing and expressing truth, goodness and beauty through relevant ways in each age and culture. In short, the communication in the Bible is indeed contextual.

Orality in Communication

As discussed, communication is central to the Bible and this centrality can be seen from the main concept of God's speech and actions to humankind and their responses to him. We must keep in mind that the Bible (especially the Hebrew Scriptures), although a literary work, was written largely for public oral recitation, not for private reading. It was composed to be heard. Reading quietly and privately to oneself was a later development. In the ancient world reading was done aloud. This is evident in the Hebrew word *qara*, "read," for it also means "call" or "shout." Even today Jews use a related term for the Bible: *miqra* ("reading aloud"). Thus understanding came through the ear, not the eye (see Alter 1981, 90; Kennedy 1984, 5-6). An oral prevalence among humans has persisted from time immemorial. Later written forms are not to be despised, but do not replace the oral. Despite a variety of electronic communication and written systems worldwide, most of the current world populations of six and half billion residents function primarily in the realm of orality (Sogaard 1993, 176). According to Dawn Herzog Jewell, more recent estimates indicate that now four billion are oral learners and "seventy percent of the world's people today can't, don't or won't read (2006, 56).

To a larger or lesser extent, "all categories of peoples of the earth" (Smith 2008, 3) have essential dimensions of oral communication. In fact, in the majority of cultures, both oral and literate, many forms of orality complement communication related to education and assist in the socialization process. Smith states:

The culture of biblical times included many oral communities. The early transmission of Scripture was by oral means for decades if not centuries. The oral languages used for the Jewish Scriptures in the Old Testament were mostly Aramaic based and/or Hebrew. For the New Testament they were spoken Aramaic and likely Koine Greek, the common language that Alexander the Great had instituted across his vast Empire from Persia to Europe from the fourth century before Christ (Ibid., 16).

Analyzing communication from the biblical perspective, mass communication in the ancient world was extremely limited and usually oral. Gideon Sjoberg believes that even the elite were dependent upon word-of-mouth for most communication in the Scriptures. For them—as well as for less literate groups—literacy was used to enhance and facilitate orality (Sjoberg 1960, 286).

Based on Sjoberg's advocacy David Cartlidge comments, "The evidence from late antiquity is that oral operations (presentation and hearing) and literary operations (reading and writing) were: inescapably interlocked and communal activities. Choreographs were created for and by the community and in the service of orality (1990, 400-401).

This was true not only of literature. Letters were not read silently by individuals, but read aloud; letters to groups would be performed orally. For this reason, P Botha believes the belief that one must reckon with the letter as having been prepared for a careful performance, and with the fact that eventually the letter was delivered like a proper speech (Botha 1992, 17-34). Textuality, when it existed, was an aid to oral presentation.

Oral Communication in the Old Testament

There are four stages of communication in Jewish cultural history: first, a patriarchal, nomadic, oral society; second, a neo-literate, tribal nation; third, a semiliterate kingdom; and last, a literate, dispersed, ethnic nationality (Litteral 1988, 1-11). In the first period, in the Old Testament, society was oral (preliterate), nomadic and organized around a patriarch. The primary religious communicative events were God speaking to humans and humans responding with prayers and sacrifices. These events were unscheduled and the settings were natural rather than in special buildings or locations. The main participants were God the initiator, and a patriarchal man of God who was the primary audience (Ibid., 2). The patriarch's role was both that of a prophet, a receiver of information from God whose communication with God was verbal, and a priest, whose communication was visual through sacrifices. He in turn communicated orally about God with others (Smith 2008, 13). The household under the patriarch was the primary social setting in which communication about God took place. Since there was no written medium then, in other periods even when the written medium was developed, the oral communication was still prevalent.

In Scripture, storytelling was common: Nathan brought conviction to David through his story of one little lamb (2 Sam 12); Samson used riddles (Judg 14:12f); and Jesus frequently spoke in parables, a pattern also found in the Old Testament (Matt 13:34; Ezek 17:2). The parables of the Good Samaritan, the Prodigal Son, or the rich man and Lazarus are noteworthy.

"Many of the prophets came from farming or shepherding backgrounds, and were likely non-literate, though some were quite literate" (Ibid., 14). In communicating to peoples in oral societies, Ezekiel employed dramatic effects such as eating the scroll (3:1-2), acting out the siege of Jerusalem (4:1-17), and demonstrating the city's desolation by cutting off his hair with a sharp sword, weighing it, burning part of it, and scattering the rest (5:1-17). These approaches would be potent among oral societies. The use of certain objects and symbols, such as the pillar of fire, the Ark of the Covenant, the two tablets of stone, Aaron's rod that budded and the brazen serpent, also had a powerful impact among such peoples.

The Passover was a significant and earthshaking event for Israel. Continuing reminders of this historic deliverance from Egypt were communicated in many ways. Primarily, the heads of Jewish families were to rehearse the works, wonders and word of God related to these events at the annual festival of Passover. Smith sees repeated reenactment of the Passover as "the confessional recital of the redemptive acts of God" (Ibid., 15). Another festival building a sense of continuity with the past is Purim, remembering Esther's salvation of the Jews from the hands of Haman, the Amalekite. Similarly, Christ's institution of communion is a clear example of continuity through oral tradition. The injunction is to remember the Lord's death till he comes. The experience of communion symbolically ties believers back into the past historical event of his death, and projects them forward to the future hope of his second appearing and return.

The oral compositions of many Psalms, probably composed during the night watches, were often set to music. They were the grounds for meditation and reflection, not only on God—his character, wonders, works and words—but also on personal responses of his servants in testimony of his protection and provision, confession of failure or repentance, and praise for restoration, sustenance and deliverance. These still speak to the hearts of humans, but especially to those with oral backgrounds.

Oral Communication in Jesus' Ministry

In Christ's day, elite religious communicators controlled the Jewish religion. Of course, he addressed people who were literate and yet were part of an essential oral culture. He preached in a way that helped his audience to remember and to repeat the message (Gittins 1989, 70-71). Some of his preaching was repetitious: "Blessed are the poor in spirit . . . ; blessed are those who mourn . . . ; blessed are the meek . . ." (Matt 5:3-11). In the Sermon on the Mount, six times Jesus also used the expression, "You have heard that it was said . . . , but I say to you . . ." (Matt 5:21-22, 27-28, 31-32, 33-34, 38-39, 43-44). Joachim Jeremias estimates that at the time of Christ less than 1% of the people met the Jewish literacy standard (1969, 11,209). All the privileged classes were below 5% of the population and 95% of the population were reckoned to be illiterate peasants and farmers. These peasants may have had some knowledge of the Hebrew that was chanted in the synagogues, but they had little access to written texts. They were derisively referred to by the Pharisees as people of the land, or peasants, because they could not read the Law. Rabbi Ebner's opinion that the elementary schools did not develop outside Jerusalem till after 100 A.D. supports this view (see Ebner 1956).

It is obvious that Jesus did read the Old Testament and knew Hebrew (Luke 4:16-19). Yet he was never a follower of any particular school of rabbinic theology so that he could not be officially recognized as a practicing Rabbi. The fact that he socialized with the common people meant he broke socially and religiously with the religious elite of his day (Klem 1978, 483). Our Lord also had a distinctive communicative style that set him apart from the official teachers of religion of his day. The Pharisees demanded that their pupils become proficient in reading the Hebrew text that lacked vowels. Only after learning to read the Law could they go on to memorize the oral laws that were also in Hebrew (Ibid., 483).

In contrast to the Pharisaic communicational policy, Jesus taught in Aramaic and apparently dropped the literacy requirement for his students. He used teaching techniques that were effective among the non-reading masses of his day. "When the sayings of Jesus are translated from our present Greek versions back into Aramaic, they are found to be poetic. Even in Greek and English many of the sayings of Jesus meet the Hebrew definition of poetry" (Burney 1925, 46). Lines of parallel thoughts form Hebrew poetic structure, and rhyming is usually avoided as a mark of vulgarity. Yet many sections of Christ's teachings in Aramaic apparently rhymed, including the Lord's Prayer, the Beatitudes, and the parable of the sheep and the goats. "The poetic structure is obviously an aid to memorization. A wide range of current New Testament scholars indicate that we need to take the poetic quality of all of Christ teachings more seriously" (Klem 1978, 483-4).

Based on the above opinions, it can be affirmed that Jesus was an oral communicator working among non-reading people in a style that identified him as one of the common people, and they heard him gladly. He taught people in a style that would facilitate easy memorization and popular transmission of his words among the common folk who did not read. He may have chanted or even sung his poems as song. Dale Jones points out the way Jesus communicated:

> The vast majority of Jesus' teachings to the crowds were in the form of parables. "Jesus spoke all these things to the crowd in parables; he did not say anything to them without using a parable" (Matt 13:34). . . . Jesus taught his disciples using the teaching style with which they were most comfortable – oral, narrative or illustrative communication (2008, 185).

According to Jones, in using oral communication, Jesus made a basic approach of locating parables with the social, cultural and religious world of his day in order to get his hearers to think and ponder what he was actually telling them. In other words, in Jesus' most characteristic teaching/preaching method parables were 'speech-acts' that had a forceful, transformative impact on his audience (or at least on those who were receptive). Like Jones, David Buttrick also comments that Jesus' parables drew on many common experiences in the lives of his hearers (2008, 431). And of course, there is also an action in parables designed to shake us and then change our minds as they were used contextually.

Erich H Keihl says that one of Jesus' most successful oral communication strategies was the use of the aesthetic elements in the parables. He captured and maintained the attention of his hearers by using such aesthetic elements as familiar characters, and scenes, contemporary forms of expressions like surprise, paradox, and sudden twist to challenge the audience's conventional values ((1990, 245). They move the audience to participate actively and act out their roles in their thoughts and actions. These elements of the parables encourage the audience to participate along with the communicator in the hermeneutic process (Leary 1986, 497). For example, the parable of the wicked tenants (Mark 12:1-2 and par.) not only maintained the attention of the audience—especially the chief priests and the Pharisees—but also enabled them to identify themselves with the character of the tenants.

Having viewed the different perceptions of key authors, it can be validated that one of the most striking features of Jesus' method of communication was his use of stories in the form of parables. In conveying the message, he invited his audience to play roles within the story, to identify with its characters and try to share in their experience as a way of interpreting the values and visions of his "received world" and making decisions accordingly. Evaluating from a communication perspective, his communication was conducted entirely within the philosophical, cultural and social orbit of the recipients. He could, therefore, fully state and demonstrate certain parts of his message, and allow other parts of his essential message to be discovered by those who were responsive enough to seek the full meaning of his words.

Some twenty years after the death and resurrection of Jesus the disciples finally felt the need to commit the sayings of Jesus to writing. "When the sayings of Jesus were finally written, it was apparently not for Aramaic churches, but for the Greek-speaking churches" (Klem 1978, 484). Certainly knowledge of the Word of God is essential for spiritual maturity. However, Jesus gave the people the Word of God in a form they could both learn and teach without passing through the needle's eye of functional literacy. The Scriptures were transmitted by memory, and the text was an aid to memory. "If there was a question about the accuracy of a written text, the rabbis gave greater authority to the accompanying oral tradition than to the written text" (Ibid., 484).

Orality in the Pauline Tradition

We have seen that most people were illiterate in the time of Jesus. In its first century of existence, Christianity was an oral phenomenon. Joanna Dewey states that:

> Literacy in Greco-Roman antiquity was limited both in the ways it was used and in the percentage of the population who were literate. People lived in an oral culture. Even the most literate would have made little use of reading or writing for either business or pleasure. On the other hand, writing was both an instrument of power and a symbol of the Roman Empire (1994, 37).

Her comment further indicates that Paul and his congregations lived in a largely oral media world, with minimal use of written texts or appeal to manuscript authority. Although Paul produced texts for long-distance correspondence, which later became authoritative texts, Christians did not yet view texts as central. 2 Thessalonians, Colossians, and Ephesians provide evidence of a developing literacy tradition; however, the Pastoral and the canonical and Apocryphal Acts seem to derive from the oral memory of Paul rather than from his letters.

Paul himself was literate, possibly because of his social class—he spoke of his craft labor as if it were choice rather than economic necessity—or because of his training as a Pharisee. He wrote more letters to the churches than anyone else in the New Testament. Literacy comes into play in his churches in four respects: "the production of letters, the reception of the letters, the possible use of Scripture in worship, and the use of Scripture in debate" (Ibid.,48). The primary use of literacy was for long distance letters, such as those written by Paul, at least one letter from Corinthian Christians to Paul (1 Cor 5:9), and letters of recommendation (2 Cor 3:1-2). Here letters are a substitute for personal presence, not the preferred means of communication, although Paul may have upon occasion deliberately chosen to write rather than to go himself, as the more effective means of influencing a community. Furthermore, as noted above, oral preparation seems to be an integral part of the creation of the written texts. Here, literacy seems definitely in the service of oral communication. While texts were produced that later became very important within Christianity as texts, these texts began as aids to orality, and seemingly had little importance in themselves.

In spite of the fact that Paul composed written letters and quoted passages from written texts in those letters, "Paul and his churches were fundamentally dependent on the oral medium and oral authority" (Ibid., 56). Only gradually did the Christian churches shift to reliance on manuscripts or texts. The endurance of the oral perspective can be seen in the textual treatments of Paul in the early second century. But by the mid-second century, both orthodox and a variety of heterodox Christian leaders were appealing to manuscripts rather than to oral tradition and authority. The oral hermeneutics of the Pauline congregations were becoming the textual hermeneutics of the church fathers. This shift was facilitated by the emergence of a hierarchical, male, educated—thus literate—church leadership and then reinforced by such leaders' use of the manuscript medium (Ibid., 56). But for the first century or so of its existence, Christianity remained predominantly an oral phenomenon, relying on oral hermeneutics and appealing to oral authority. The Paul of this church was the Paul whose life and work could be recalled to memory, not yet the Paul chiefly apprehended through letters.

The whole Bible is the story of the communication of God with people, and of people with their fellows. Out of a variety of modes and methods of communication, as we have seen, orality is appropriate for all cultures:

oral, non-literate, semi-literate and highly literate. First, in all peoples and cultures family network structures include many generations, giving a strong sense of continuity and connectedness. Second, much of the early socialization and domestic education is carried on through oral means in the home and local community. Even where, in some societies as time goes by, the emphasis changes more to literate media, the oral bridges to extensive relationships continue to exist in most of the world. Recognizing the prevalence of the oral communication in the Bible, what can we use from insight gained for communicating the gospel to the Burmese Buddhists in Yangon?

Using Oral Tools for Communicating Mission

There are different tools for communication in different cultures and ages in the Bible. However, I will focus only on memorization and recitation as sample tools in the biblical context. The rationale is that the use of these communication tools can be relevantly applied in the context of Burmese Buddhists.

Memorizing Scripture is a matter of course in most of the world's religions (Coward 1988, 117-118). In the Old Testament times, homes, synagogues, schools and courts were the important centers for the preservation and continuation of tradition. At home, a child grew in an atmosphere which was conducive to learning in the oral tradition. That is why for the Jews memorizing Torah was "sweeter than honey, more precious than gold" (Klem 1982, 63-67). When boys went to school, there again the transmission of the "oral Torah" took place rigorously. In fact, the oral Torah had to be preserved and passed on in oral form. Living books were the transmitters of oral Torah. For the importance of memorization in oral tradition, Briger Gerhardsson states it in this way:

> A well-known tradition tells of R Hiyya the elder that if the Torah should be forgotten in Israel he would proceed in the following way: he would buy seeds of flax, plant them, reap the flax, and make ropes, with which he would capture some

hinds; from their skins he would then make scrolls on which he would write (from memory) the Torah (Pentateuch). Then he would go to a town where there was no teacher, and there teach five boys to read a book each from the Pentateuch, and teach six other boys to repeat a *mishnah* order each. The boys would then be able to teach one another (1961, 114).

In ancient educational theory the assumption was that words and items of knowledge must be memorized. In learning to recite the oral Torah, they used two basic principles. One was that the material is memorized, the other that the concern for understanding the meaning of the text was addressed only after they had learned the text by heart.

While Gerhardsson stresses the importance of memorization as the basic form of oral transmission, but involving more than verbatim memorization, Werner Kelber argues that this verbatim memorization as a key factor in oral transmission has been abandoned by the majority of experts, and oral transmission is controlled by the law of social identification rather than by the technique of verbatim memorization (1983, 27). According to these two authors, the consistency and continuity of oral transmission have been prevalent since the Old Testament time. This is similar to differing scenery, which may change along a riverbank, but the primary flow of the stream stays constant and its direction remains the same. Oral peoples rely heavily on memory. Which is likely to be more from hearing sources and certain contextual visual associations, than from written or script forms.

In the New Testament time, in a milieu of a predominant illiteracy, the incarnation of Jesus Christ took place and thus the gospel story was developed in an oral form before being written down. Jesus operated in the communications world of orality. Although he could read, he did not write any of his teachings, but taught his disciples to recite from memory. Most of the early church members were oral or semi-literate people including slaves, the poor, the downtrodden and the disenfranchised. Theological examples from the history of the era and in the New Testament text indicate that orality played a significant role in the spread of the church and in the nurturing of the believers who often lived in harsh environments (Klem 67/268: 1978, 479-484). "Creeds such as the Nicene Creed, spiritual hymns, psalms, invocations, prayers and benedictions were committed to memory and repeatedly used" (Smith 2008, 15). Public reading of Scripture without comment made God's Word available to the oral masses (Luke 4:16-21). Paul commanded Timothy to practice this (1 Tim 4:13).

According to the history of Buddhism, the Buddha used his own language of Maghadi in the early spread of his teaching. At his death in 486 BC, the first Buddhist Council called upon Ananda, one of his five closest disciples, to recite from memory the whole teaching of the Buddha. Much of the content of Buddhist scriptures was based on oral sources (Coward 1988, 146-148) and by oral communication; Buddhism crossed borders and influenced nations. Today, the oral mechanism for transmitting the gospel message to Buddhists is primarily through links, ladders and bridges, which enable the Christian communicator to cross over to those cultures by means of their myths, legends, stories, parables, wisdom sayings, and local tales.

All social classes use storytelling. Every people and culture has common memories, a history, and identity. This common identity has to be passed on to each generation. This is normally done through storytelling. A story does not need to be read from a book. It can be proclaimed, recited from memory, dramatized or sung, for people have a common identity when they share the same stories. The content and form of stories, as well as the manner and time of telling them, may differ considerably. But according to Gittins, "storytelling itself is a means to assure group identity and also to exclude those who do not belong. Whether they are myths or fables, histories or biographies, genealogies or legends, our stories define who we are and what we believe, where we find meaning" (1989, 72-73). In the Bible we hear God's story, a story which has become our own. In Jesus of Nazareth, the universal story of humankind is present in the story of one particular individual.

In the Buddhist scriptures, much of the content of *Tripitaka* was based on oral sources. First, the *Jatakas* were the stories of the previous incarnations of the Buddha. At least 550 *Jataka* of his former birth stories, now in print, were passed down orally during the early centuries. They are tales with a precise literary format and structure. They are interesting stories meant to keep the audience's attention in communication of Buddhism.

Buddhist missionaries told stories. In Myanmar whenever Buddhist monks preach in the public square, they use stories as a means of communication. According to Miriam Adeney, telling stories is an effective medium in Buddhism as stories touch at multiple levels, "affecting not only our cognition but also our senses and emotions" (2008, 87-89). Further, they lead our imaginations from one discovery to another as the more we participate in these discoveries, the more we remember.

Summary

As discussed, the nature of the Bible is communication in both the Old and New Testaments. This central task of God's self-communication always occurs in the cultural contexts of the audience throughout the Bible. As God is by nature the perfect communicator, this communicational task originated in the Triune God and from the communication within the Trinity God reaches out to His creatures. He creates human beings in his own image and likeness, which means being able to communicate and live in a communicative community. He then speaks and reveals himself to these human beings beginning with Adam and then throughout their history with Israel. The incarnation of Jesus Christ is the high point and fullness of God's self-communication, in his Son becoming one of us and communicating the love of the Father to all human beings. As the agent of his communication, his church begins this task of communication with the coming of the Holy Spirit as the agent of God's self-communication. This ongoing self-communication of God through the church is to carry on till the end of the age to all nations including Burmese Buddhists in Yangon. But awareness of the background of reference of the target audience is essential for effective communication. Like Jesus, Buddha also frequently adopted this method of being mindful of a receiver's context before he communicated his message. (Ariyadasa 2005, 69-70). Thus, contextual communication with Burmese Buddhists in Yangon should interact with their cultural, religious, social, political, and economic context. We will discuss these issues in chapter 3.

CHAPTER 3

Socio-Cultural Religious Context of the Burmese in Yangon City

Myanmar with its total population of nearly 60 million is made up of 135 national ethnic groups. Of these the main groups are 70% Burmese, 1.2% Chin, 1.4% Kachin, less than 1% Kayeh, 8.9% Kayin, 2% Mon, 5% Rakhine and 10% Shan (Kaung VII 3/ 2002, 26). These groups can be distinguished by tracing their ethnic-linguistic stock into "three major categories: (1) Tibeto-Burman stock which comprises Burmese, Rakhine (Arakanese), Chin, Kachin; (2) Sino-Tibetan stock which comprises Kayin, Kayah, Shan, and (3) Austro-Asiatic stock comprises Mon and others. In this multi-ethnic diversity of the country, Yangon is the largest city with political, social and socio-economic influences as well as religious significance, located at the convergence of the Yangon and Bago Rivers about 19 miles (30 km) from the Gulf of Mottama. Presently, the Yangon city territorial limits cover an area of 236.342 square miles (Yangon Development Committee 1999, 77). The government has been developing the city intensively, and needless to say, the urban society of Yangon is also increasingly modernized with about six million people—the majority being the Burmese Buddhists.

A Brief History of the Burmese People

In order to communicate the gospel meaningfully and to serve effectively as God's prophetic agent calling for the conversion and transformation of people, societies, and cultures, the church must know the socio-cultural and historical contexts in which it lives and ministers. An understanding of the contexts or frameworks will obviously differ from person to person and from country to country. If we are to communicate the gospel to the Burmese Buddhists in Yangon city, it is essential to understand the context in which they live and in which their interaction with the gospel takes place. In the words of David Filbeck:

> For a *communicator* (italics mine) to understand communication, especially cross-cultural communication, he/she must first understand the basis on which communication takes place . . . What is the foundation on which a message is transmitted and received? More precisely, where does a person begin in communicating with another, and on what basis does the other person receive and interpret the communication? The answer is to be found in the way society, of both the communicator and the receiver, is organized. The social organization of the participants, in other words, forms the foundation which underlines communication, the transmission and receiving of messages from one person to another (1985, 3).

The early history of the Burmese is little known, but reliable historical resources tell something of their mythical past, which has influenced their self-understanding. Most Christian scholars who wrote histories of Myanmar churches from *ethnic* perspectives emphasized Buddhism and Burmese culture when searching for a reason for the Burmese's non-responsiveness to the true gospel. They almost left the early history of Burmese people out of their research. In some accounts, we may come across an overview of Burmese history, but we do not encounter details that lead us to understand the Burmese passion which they experience in their lives. As we delve into Burmese history, we will realize why they are resisting Christianity. Most scholars and missionaries until today agree that as Buddhism is deeply rooted in the Burmese mind, Christian teaching is not able to communicate with them. But on the other hand, it is also 'their nationalism' which closes the Burmese eyes from seeing the light of

Christ. In reality, Buddhism is merely a platform used for nationalism. If we analyze the primitive accounts of these Burmese people, we will realize why they are serious about their nation and how they became nationalists. There are various factors which have caused the Burmese people to become nationalists to protect themselves from Christianity.

The earliest historical experience of the Burmese people was the foundation which over time created a nationalistic attitude. Even though it is impossible to say what the pre-historic account of Myanmar was, most the historians agree that the original Burmese were a tribe of Mongolians or the Tibeto-Burmese (in Chinese it is known as *Mien*) from the southeastern slopes of Tibet who migrated into Myanmar. Professor Than Tun, a Burmese historian, concluded that the Burmese's original home might have been the northwest of China, from the Han dynasty (2004, 123-131; see also Aung 1967, 231).

As they were forced out by the Chinese, they took refuge in northeast Tibet and since they were incessantly persecuted by Nanchao, they then entered the plains of Myanmar in 751-794 (Tun 1988, 3). According to Maung Htin Aung, the Tibeto-Burmese people were culturally well developed, as were the Chinese and Tibetans at the time. Since these two great kingdoms, China and Tibet, were rivals the Tibeto-Burmese became sandwiched between them. Thus, "they considered their independence and social institutions to be more valuable than their material culture." Finally they ran away from their homeland and migrated into Myanmar (1967, 2-3). With regard to the period of migration of Burmese people, D G E Hall states:

> So far as reliable records are concerned, the period from the middle of the ninth to the middle of the eleventh centuries is a blank. This is all the more unfortunate since it was during this period that Burmese entered Burma. Their original home seems to have been somewhere in the northwest of China, probably Kansu, between the Gobi Desert and northeast Tibet. The earliest Chinese written records, coming from the latter half of the second millennium BC, call them the Ch'iang. Chinese hostility forced them to take refuge in

> northeast Tibet. In the first millennium BC they were pursued by the Chinese rulers of Ts'in through the mountains towards the south. There we lose sight of them for a long period until they reappear many centuries later among the Mang tribes under the suzerainty of Nanchao. To escape from the dominance of Nanchao they entered the plains of Burma, coming down through the region between the 'Nmai Hka and the Salween and ultimately setting in the Kyaukse district (1956, 11).

Hence, we can assume that these people had long been displaced people. They probably longed to settle down and establish skills and would have tried to find an opportunity to build a great nation for themselves and their people.

Another account can be found in the Myanmar Chronicle which tells that the earliest dwellers of Myanmar were the *Pyus* (Ibid., 8) whose kingdom was in *Sri Ksetra*. The Burmese people had founded a small settlement of their own while supporting and merging with the *Pyus*. The Pyu capital had fallen to Nanchao raids and three thousand *Pyus* were taken away in captivity to *Yunan Fu* in 832 AD When the Nanchao raids ceased, the Burmese people felt themselves strong enough to build a fortified city of their own (Aung 1967, 30-31).

Emergence of Nationalism

In AD 1044, Anawrahtar was enthroned, and he was the first king of Pagan dynasty. The guilding framework of the modern Burmese state was laid at Bagan, the first Burmese empire, traditionally dated AD 1057-1287 through king Anawrahtar (Thwin 1985, 199). Using a strengthened army, he brought stability and unity to his kingdom. His greatest achievement in bringing the various tribes into a single nation was significant in history. Here the Burmese nationalistic attitude rapidly appeared under his reign because he was careful to look after his own people. He showed his Burmese people to the Chinese as *Pyus* who had recently fallen by Nanchao. "Thus the Chinese, for a long while, were not aware of the change of leadership in

Burma" (Aung 1967, 37). From that time onwards, whenever their kingdom was threatened and almost destroyed, there was always another king who could re-establish a new Burmese kingdom. These significant aspects of continuity persist with echoes of traditional values resonating within contemporary Burmese politics. As legacies, they continue to reverberate within notions of kingship and statecraft, in patterns of power and authority, and in their relationship with Buddhist concept.

The history of Burmese people shows how they developed into a ruling nation. They subdued the tribes and nations that were within the boundaries of Myanmar and ruled over them for centuries. They were also a regional power as king after king attacked and conquered neighboring countries as far as Manipur and Thailand. During *Bayintnaung's* reign, Myanmar had the largest army in Southeast Asia. King *Sinbyusin* was victorious even over the invading Chinese army (see Bunge 1983). The noteworthy historical past gave the Burmese a distinctive national pride. This naturally makes the Burmese feel superior to other nations, including Westerners.

Buddhism as Nationalism

During the reign of Burmese kings, King Anawrahtar with the help of his spiritual advisor Shin Arahan, implanted the Theravada form of Buddhism. He totally suppressed and banished *Aris*, a lawless group of Mahayana Buddhist monks. The people, obsessed as they had been by the faith of the Aris and other indigenous religious rites and practice, now envisaged a new order of life, and with this great acquisition opened a new chapter in the religious life of the people. From then onward, for the Burmese people Theravada Buddhism stood as the national religion, and its propagation throughout the realm mean the kingdom rapidly became a great center of religion and culture (Lubeigt 2004, 236). It can be seen that the Burmese fusion of their national and religious identity took its roots in the long historical and traditional development from the founding of the first Burmese dynasty. Accordingly, the influence of Buddhism on the Burmese people is so strong and pervasive that they identify the nationalism with the religion as one identity. That is why the Burmese Buddhists cannot think of nationhood apart from Buddhism as it welded the Burmese together, like two faces of the same coin. Consequently, when a Burmese Buddhist converted to another religion, he was considered to have put away his Burmese blood and became non-Burmese.

After the first, second and third Anglo-Burmese Wars, the whole country of Myanmar came under the British colonial rule. The abolition of kingly rule was a heavy blow to Buddhism. In the traditional structure of Myanmar, the king performed a lot of functions in the promotion of Buddhism. When the British conquered the whole country, some might assume that Burmese nationalism would be crushed (Nawl 2004, 17). On the contrary, Buddhism became a uniting force of nationalism against the British. In other words, British colonial rule fanned the flame of nationalism into a greater conflagration. Buddhist nationalism was expressed through many movements and groups. In 1906 the Young Men's Buddhist Association (YMBA) was formed among newly educated young urban Burmese to promote Buddhism and Burmese culture. They addressed political questions under the British rule (Cady 1966, 189). There were strikes by university and high school students, and Buddhist monks under the leadership of U Ottama, agitated for self-rule. The YMBA changed its name to the General Council of Burmese Association (GCBA) and organized *Wunthanu Athins* (*Wunthanu* Association) which established political associations at the village level (Win 1988, 270-279). Seriously speaking, Buddhism is still an important figure in the national heritage and is both the symbol and the essential feature of its national identity as well.

Since the times of the kings, the monks and laymen of the Burmese Buddhists have acknowledged the religious function of the kings as the promoters of Buddhism and of the *Sangha* (order of monks). Under the British, Buddhism had no defender, promoter and protector. However, after independence under the democratic government Prime Minister U Nu declared, "It was the responsibility of the government to look after the welfare of the people not only in the present existence but in countless future existence and that it was therefore necessary to make Buddhism the State religion of Burma" (Smith 1965, 25-26). Like the ancient kings, with strong determination U Nu tried to adopt Buddhism as the state religion.

In 1962 General Ne Win seized power from the Democratic government and set up the Revolutionary Government of the Union of Burma. In 1964, Ne Win's government nationalized the Christian mission schools and mission hospitals and dispensaries. In line with this nationalization foreign missionaries were asked to leave the country in 1966. This political Buddhist-nationalistic spirit of the government predominates till now under the State Peace and Development Council incepted in 1988. This Buddhist-nationalism has been a challenge for the communication of the gospel which came through the colonizing countries.

Social Organization of the Burmese People

The term social organization refers to the systematic ordering of social relations by acts of choice and decision. These acts are guided by precedents that are provided by the social structure and limited by the range of possible alternatives (Jha 2003, 41, 44). Thus, observable behavior, including change and variation in a social system, is accounted for in its social organization, and the total pattern of social organization within a culture serves to maintain orderly relationships among individuals and groups. In reality, of course, it forms the basic underlying contextual communication of the gospel within a specific society (Filbeck 1985, 5).

Social Classes in Burmese Societies

An understanding of contemporary Burmese society is incomplete without the study of their social structure and cultural and religious values. Burmese society may be characterized as "kinship society, whereas the society from which Europe or America is a modern society" (Jha 2003, 49-50; Filbeck 1985, 34). All agree that there is no society without social grouping or collectivities. These differences in the sociological base of communication must be taken into consideration when a paradigm of contextual Christian communication is designed. In particular, it is important to remember that although the gospel is addressed not to society but to individuals, these people are individuals in a society. For this reason W A Haviland says, "There is no society without individuals" (1993, 31). According to Haviland's statement, any communicating information can be received and interpreted both on the basis of how society is organized and how an individual has interacted with his or her social organization.

To study the concept of social classes in Burmese societies, we need to revisit some of their traditional concepts. The reason is that Burmese society is very widely known as a traditional-bound conservative society so much that many, if not all, of the traditional wisdoms, concepts and ideas still prevail today and exert strong influence in every facet of life of the Burmese. An attempt to understand the social context of the development of modern Burmese society is not comprehensive unless the traditional customs, concepts and behavior are taken into account. A basic knowledge of the traditional cultural concepts of these people and society is therefore important especially in the context of Christian communication.

The traditional Myanmar thinking and concepts recognize class differences and class discrimination according to the chronicles of Myanmar. Before the British colonized Myanmar, four distinct social classes sustained society: "*Min-myo* (Mahasamata and his descendents, or the kattia class), *Ponnar-myo* (Brahmins class), *Thuhtay-Thugwye-myo* (the wealthy class), and *Thusinye-myo* (the poor class)" (Soe 2005, 134). Later, however, they eventually divided social classes into five categories: "farmers (or cultivators), merchants (or traders), entrepreneurs, well-informed and reputed *hmu-matts* or royal officials, *nowadays they can be regarded as relatives of generals of Junta as there is no more monarchy in the country*, (italics mine), and the learned revered monks" (Ibid.,134-135). An understanding of these differences is of great importance for effective communication of the gospel to the Burmese in all three phases of conversion. How and where can the communicators meet them with the gospel? What are the economic implications of a decision to become a Christian? What would be the livelihood of these Burmese after they have become Christians? Questions like these, which form the background for an analysis of a Burmese Buddhist society, are crucial for the development of contextual Christian communication to the Burmese Buddhists in Yangon today. Further, whatever their social class, Burmese people are family-oriented. So in this section instead of tracing each different social class, I will concentrate only on the social values of family networks in "the Burmese urban societal context" as these values directly influence the process of communication of the gospel.

Burmese Social Values

Regardless of social classes, the social values of the Burmese people in Myanmar form the relational attitude of the Burmese and control how they relate to others in their community and society. In addition, these values specify the standard and mode of conduct for individuals in their daily life throughout Burmese society. In this section, I consider six kinds of Burmese social values and analyze it from the contextual issues in communication.

The Burmese people are a very cultured people. Among the strongest of Burmese social values is that of paying respect to and/or deferring to one's parents, elders, and superiors. That is why respect for old age and obedience to elders, parents and teachers are strictly observed in speech and behavior. M H L Cing states:

> In terms of verbal communication, different sets of pronouns and patterns of speech are used for different genders, age, status, as well as on the relatedness and degree of closeness between the speaker (first person pronoun) and the listener (second person pronoun). Misuse of personal pronoun is not only disgraceful for the speaker but also very offensive to the one addressed. Thus, it is very important to use the correct form of address. Communication with the monks calls for an entirely different set of vocabulary. Good manners and respectful attitudes are crucial elements in Burmese interpersonal relationships. In the presence of elders one has to stand with heads bowed, walk in a stooping attitude, sit neatly, and if possible, the toes must not be pointing at the elder person. In short, the body language must reveal respect and humility. To question, disgrace, or argue with elders including parents and teachers is considered a very despicable act. The younger person is expected to listen quietly and to obey the elder person. Table manners are also observed by well-bred Burmese. Nobody touches the food unless the eldest in the family first takes a spoonful from some of the dishes into his or her plate (2001, 89).

Cing's statement points out how the interpersonal relationship among the Burmese Buddhist society is integrated in terms of communication verbally and non-verbally. This integration is highly regarded as the value of Burmese influencing any social class. Professor Hla Pe adds:

> Burmese Buddhists are conservative and sticklers for the tradition that has been handed down from generation to generation. They nourished the attitude that "what was good enough for my parents is good enough for me. This tradition which acts as guideline in their course of life encourages discipline, respect and humility, and thoughtfulness (1985, 166).

Secondly, being in the patron-client or subordinate-superior relationship offers security and protection as well as economic benefit for Burmese individuals. His relationship with his patron, superior, or "older brother" will ensure his survival and the achievement of his goals. These relationships are to be reciprocal by nature and require exchanges between the patron and the client. Rubin J Herbert argued that the patron-client relationship or the older-to-younger relationship in Thais can change depending upon the circumstances. Although Herbert's argument concerned Thais, it could be applied to the Burmese as well.

> The patron, from a position of economic security, offers tangible goods such as economic aid and protection. In return, the client, from a position of economic insecurity, offers more intangible goods. These include loyalty, a commitment to increasing the good name of his patron, information and political support . . . Also, there may be several hierarchal levels of patron-client relations. Patrons at lower levels are themselves clients of higher level patrons who, in turn, are clients of still higher level patrons (1973, 273).

Based on above statement, we can ascertain that the social relationships in Burmese society are organized around factions that are formed along kinship lines and by patronage. This poses difficulties for introducing new ideas or concepts that would require Burmese people to change patronage or entourage. So the social value which places important consideration for patron-client relationships, also holds an important position in the Burmese' "value system." In this relationship, the patron provides support, protection, and advice, while the client or inferior will offer loyalty, respect, and honor. The decision-making authority is deferred to the patron or superior.

Third is the importance of family networks or solidarity of the household. The word 'family' refers to the social institution in which members are incorporated. For any society, it is the natural and "fundamental social unit established by a man and woman who live together, who co-operate economically, and who produce and rear children. In harmony with this family has often been viewed as a residential unit" (Taylor 1973, 255). According to Taylor, no matter how independent and basic this nuclear family unit is, it also has strong connected links through its extended family networks associated with the partners. In Burmese culture, this family network is broader than in industrialized states, being incorporated into structures of clans, tribes, consolidated communities and sometimes nations. Donald McGavran advocates that faith flows in "closed family ties or tightly knit webs of relationships and many extended families. He saw extended families had a close blood and marriage web" (1970, 174). These webs of relationships are organisms composed of individuals closely and permanently linked together. Any society is instituted with families, and of course, anthropologists, sociologists and psychologists recognize many different ways of viewing basic human interaction, expressed through societal family networks.

In the social organization of marriage and family, Taylor suggests two distinctions of basic importance, social group and social category. The former is defined by actual interaction among the members who perform roles in relation to one another and the latter by something the members have in common, independently of whether or not members interact with one another. From the sociological point of view the basis of human interaction and communication revolves around various statuses and roles, as well as other components like kinship and sex differences, which develop a consciousness of kind or identity (1973, 243). In this regard, family helps consolidate individuals into a sociological if not biological kin and value group, and gives one identity in society. It also provides the means for nurture, protection and provision for the members' survival. To communicate the gospel effectively, it is necessary for Protestant Christian communicators to understand how a family functions in the Burmese social context.

In terms of marriage, the decision to choose a bride can be made by the individual; however, once a couple has decided to marry, they must consult their respective parents. With the parents' assistance, an *aungthwedaw* (an older of one's kin group) is chosen to serve as 'marriage broker' for each side. The *aungthwedaw*, usually a male, will make a decision on the bridal price and will discuss the suitability of the proposed marriage. A negotiator, who usually is a paternal uncle or a paternal grandfather for the male's side and a maternal grandfather on the female's side, will also represent each side. The most important matter to agree upon in advance is the bridal price. If there are no objections, a day and hour for the wedding is fixed upon, and the marriage is carried out (Yoe 1963, 54). According to the old system, the young man was not considered of age to marry till he was twenty-four or twenty-five. The age of the girl was always a matter of no consequence as long as she had attained puberty. Nowadays, such formalities are almost entirely dispensed with. If the parents of both houses agree, the contracting parties get married with most ardent lover-like rapidity. The age, too, has become varied. Eloping is common enough, and though the parents may be angry, they are usually too easy-going and indolent to take any energetic action in the matter, and let the couple find out their mistake and come and ask for pardon and a house to live in, which is seldom refused.

In terms of family structure, according to M Nash's field research, the family and household system of Burmese society can be classified into three types. These are: the conjugal family of father, mother, unmarried children (nuclear family); the extended conjugal family, in which a son or a daughter has formed a conjugal family and is co-resident with the father and mother and jurally subordinate to the father's-mother's family; and the joint conjugal family, in which relatives such as siblings or cousins or in-laws live in the same compound with coordinate jural status between the families (1965, 44). Based on Nash's research, Cing rightly claims that the second and third types are common among the Burmese people, and in family life the woman plays a significant role and largely influences decision-making (2001, 88). On the other hand, Aung Mang and Samuel Ngun Ling argue that the Burmese family is an extended form with interdependent relationship, authority, and responsibility networks inherent within the group. While men exercise nominal authority within the family unit, most important decisions are shared by husbands and wives. Outside the family, however, men tend to dominate (Mang 2007, 89-103; Ling 2007, 68).

In terms of the responsibilities of the members of the household in Burmese society, the male serves as household head in a position of authority over female groups. The members of the household have domestic duties or responsibilities toward one another. The parents' responsibility is to teach the children to make merit. Their role can be described as "to restrain their children from evil, to encourage them to do good, to give them education and professional training, to arrange suitable marriages for the children, and to hand over property as inheritance to them at the proper time" (Htay and Tin 2002, 150-151). The children are responsible to reciprocate by helping their parents in every way and as much as possible, to be trustworthy and good stewards in order to be recipients of their possessions, to respect and not disgrace them, to take care of them in their old age, and to continue observing religious traditions and customs so that the children can make merit for them after their death (Cing 2001, 86). Mothers, being submissive to fathers, play important roles in many aspects of Myanmar societal life. They are strictly bound by patriarchal traditions and cultures, not only to bear and care for children, but also to control the purse, prepare food, keep order and discipline, to be responsible for the general wellbeing of the whole family, and to share what she can with her husband's relations and her own (Ling 2007, 68). One concept is that women are inferior to men because they are not eligible for Buddhahood. However, others refute this idea as originating from an old Hindu custom; they say that Gautama's teaching did not contain any racial or sexual discrimination. Ling argues in this way:

> In society, the constitution gives women equal rights with men, although the Buddhist culture provides the reverse. Article 154 of the 1974 State Constitution stated that women

are allowed to enjoy equal political, economic, social and cultural rights. The Myanmar Buddhist Law also gives Myanmar women equal rights as men with regard to inheritance and divorce (Ibid.).

In Burmese society there has never been any caste system or distinction between the male and the female in matters of inheritance, ownership of property, voting rights, business and job attainment. Thus, in the family, husband and wife are seen as equal partners. Even when a Burmese woman marries, she does not have to take her husband's name, nor does she have to use her father's: she retains her own name all her life (Nyo 2000, 120-121). Marriage is only a public declaration that the couple wish to be husband and wife, not for discrimination of gender.

The fourth social value of Burmese people is social harmony. Good feelings within households, kin groups, and communities are extremely desirable among the Burmese people, who will do whatever it takes to create and maintain social harmony at all levels. This kind of social value is indeed influenced by Buddhist teachings. So strong is the feeling for social harmony even in urban context that any action taken to maintain harmony is justified and upheld by the society. Cing calls this concept *na-le-hmu* (understanding). She says, "Basically, *na-le-hmu* is good word, associated with understanding. The term also involves care and concern for the wellbeing of others" (2001, 92). This definition of social harmony indicates avoidance of confrontation or conflict. Further, it also expresses the Burmese cultural value on maintaining harmony.

Fifthly, as pointed out, Burmese people belong to a kinship society, but they are surrounded by and interact with modern societies, particularly in Yangon city, where the Burmese children are influenced by the modern society. Here the question arises how can an educational program play to the needs of Burmese Buddhists? The Burmese people place a high value on education. In the distant past, persons were honored and respected not so much for wealth as for wisdom, although this has changed somewhat nowadays. In the schools young children are taught stories from the Buddhist scriptures, about the preciousness of wisdom and learning. There are sayings which encourage learning (Ibid., 93). Here are a few examples:

Pyin-nya hu-thi myat-shwe-oh, ou-saa hu-thi myet-hleh-myo: Wisdom/knowledge is like a pot of gold; riches are like magic (i.e. riches can vanish as if like magic).

Pyin-nya shwe-oh lu ma khol: Widsom/knowledge is precious like a pot of gold but which men cannot steal. *Pyin-nya ye-yin, pwe le tint*: The wise/learned man is outstanding in the public. Nowadays, with "four social objectives" for building up the modern country, the Ministry of Education is the main provider of education in the Union of Myanmar and is functioning with the vision to create an education system that will generate a learning society capable of facing the challenges of the Knowledge Age. The Ministry of Education is implementing short- and long-term education development plans to develop a lifelong learning society. This plan is not only bringing about the enhancement of the quality of higher education and promoting diversity, but it has also markedly increased accessibility to higher education (Ministry of Education 2004, 1). Accordingly, in the modern society, which increasingly influences all ethnic groups in Yangon in particular, the content to be transmitted is Western education, which makes the individual into a modern citizen through the medium of Burmese and English. The main agent is the schoolteacher, and the learning takes place in the city schools. Some Burmese boys and girls receive at least a partial modern Western education, which helps them to survive when later in life they have to interact with the institutions of the modern Burmese society.

Last but not least, when trying to comprehend the socio-cultural context of Burmese people, the economics of the society is another feature to be considered. Looking at Myanmar, it is a rich agricultural country with abundant natural resources, the land itself offering the hope of a prosperous future. The economy has been built on agriculture, which is now being surpassed by exports from substantial natural gas reserves. The country is the world's largest exporter of teak; is one of the world's principal sources of rubies, sapphires, jade, and pearls; and is known for its tin, tungsten, and silver production. The country possesses extensive regions with rich soil and good rainfall suitable for highly productive agriculture, with major river systems allowing irrigation in many other regions. With a population density considerably lower than that of most of its regional neighbors, agricultural prosperity is definitely possible. Indeed, during its colonial heyday in the 1920s and 1930s, Myanmar was the world's leading source of rice, earning it the nickname "the rice bowl of Asia" (Perry 2007, 51) and making it home to some of the most productive and prosperous paddy farmers in the world. Yet, despite this potential prosperity, Myanmar today is impoverished by conflict, inept policies, and international isolation. Consequently, Myanmar has been in economic crisis largely. It was estimated that the annual GDP was US$ 280 per capita in 2008, or little under US$ 0.77 per day. Overall, even though Burmese people constitute 70% of the country population, they are the poorest people group in the country.

Historic Influences on the Burmese Worldview

Every social group has a worldview which is a set of more or less systematized beliefs and values through which they evaluate and attach meaning to reality. There is a range of definitions of worldview. I will follow Kraft who defines it as,

> the totality of the culturally structured images and assumptions (including value and commitment or allegiance assumptions) in terms of which a people both perceive and respond to reality. Worldview is not separate from culture. It is included in culture as the structuring deepest level pictures and presuppositions on which people base their lives (2008, 12).

According to Kraft, a people's worldview, more than any other aspect of their culture, affects communication. No one cultural group, however, can claim to have the correct worldview; rather, each group's worldview stands on its own. For the Burmese people, they see themselves as the descendants of Buddha's clan and assume that they know more about life and religion than any other ethnic group in the world (Bischoff 1995, 4). For this reason, when Western missionaries came and preached the gospel to them, they felt insulted instead of accepting it. They could not endure to hear any better knowledge than they had because they believed that they had arrived on this earth earlier than others. That is why they do not have a high regard for any other people as they highly esteem themselves.

In the context of Christian communication, Burmese people do not have a high regard for Westerners. The probable reason is when these Westerners entered the land of Myanmar, Burmese people called them *Kala Phyu*, simply meaning White Indians. Why? Because the only foreigners they obviously knew were Indians. So the white men were conveniently called *Kala Phyu*, Kala being the colloquial name for Indians when people are not in a respectful mood towards them. What King Thibaw, the last king of the country, says clearly illustrates an attitude of the Burmese people toward the Westerners. To him, the British were barbarians reflecting the attitude of the Burmese nation toward Westerners. They are superior and do not expect to learn anything from barbarians. Thus, the question in Myanmar would not be, "Why did the Burmese people not accept when they heard the gospel?" Rather, the question should be, "Did the Burmese even pay attention to what the Christians preached?" This lack of respect for the Westerners, especially after the colonization of Myanmar, is one of the reasons why so few Burmese have become Christians till now.

In addition, Westerners are also regarded as animals according to Shway Yoe. Yoe was writing not about their attitude towards the British, but about the necessity for every Burmese male to join the monkhood. He related that for a Burmese male who has not been in the monkhood at least once in life, his present existence is not as pure human being but as an animal. It would be better for that person to have been born an animal or an Englishman. Thus they place the British on the same level as the animals (1963, 19). Yoe writes: "The best thing a Burmese can wish for a good Englishman is that in some future existence, as a reward of good work, he may be born a Buddhist and if possible a Burmese" (Ibid., ix). This implies that the Englishman is in a very low state of existence now, and that the Burmese Buddhist is in the highest state.

Burmese Religious Values

The word culture is used in the sense of refinement of thought and activity in human life. This term is very wide in its significance. But if culture is to amount to anything worth having and really worthy of the name, it must be spiritually based (Thittila 2000, 215). Significantly, with Asians in general and particularly in Myanmar, the culture has been, and still is, spiritually based and a part of, not apart from, their religions. From the earliest history of the nation, Buddhism has been part of Burmese identity and culture. Thus, the Buddhist way of living is taught from childhood to the end of life pervading the very fabric of life of Burmese Buddhists' thoughts, speech and deeds. That is why Buddhism has been so integral a part of Burmese ethos as to say: "To be a Burmese is to be a Buddhist." The Burmese prominent monk Thittila claims that, "the genuine culture of Asia is based entirely on the spiritual principles of its religions. Take away our religion and what of culture is left? Just what would be left if you took away from the lotus the life-giving waters . . . nothing but the odor of decay" (Ibid., 213). Therefore, in Asian countries, the development of culture and development of religion are inseparable. D L Stults asserts, "to name a certain culture is to imply that is of a certain religious orientation" (1989, 106). In the Myanmar context, therefore, Buddhism influences its followers and is also considered as a guide to their daily life. The impact of religion in society, thus, has been very strong from generation to generation (Kaung 2002, 24-25).

Philosophically, Buddhism is quite elaborate and intricately involved. However, most Burmese people in Yangon do not perceive or practice "philosophical Buddhism or *Nibbanic* Buddhism" even though they still claim faithfulness to it. Rather, they practice Popular Buddhism or what Spiro calls "*Kammatic* Buddhism," which has a tremendous influence upon their worldview and daily life (Spiro, 11-12, 66-67, 70, 453). Thus, instead of approaching the subject of Buddhism philosophically, I will deal with it from a practical standpoint.

The authentic Buddhists take refuge in Three Incomparable Gems known as the Buddha, *Dhamma* and Sangha to guide their noble conduct. They are known as "*Saranagamana*" in Pali. It means these three Gems are taken as their refuges. The reason is that they give devotees real spiritual pleasure and happiness, and therefore they take the three Gems as their guides and refuges against the evil power of ignorance, greed, hatred and ill will (Thittila 2000, 207). So everyday a Buddhist including monks and nuns recite the formula of the three refuges before their daily religious activities start:

Buddham saranam gacchami in Pali:
I go to the Buddha for refuge;

Dhammam saranam gacchami in Pali:
I go to the Dhamma for refuge;

Sangham saranam gacchami in Pali:
I go to the Sangha for refuge.

This formula of recitation means that Buddhists go to the Buddha for refuge because "he had boundless compassion for weakness, sorrow, disappointment and suffering of human beings, and because he found for them the path of deliverance by his own ceaseless effort through countless lives. He has given them great encouragement and inspiration to fight against evil until they overcome it" (Ibid., 207-208). Thus, he is their supreme teacher who shows the correct way to happiness, welfare and liberation, and he himself is completely pure, perfect in thought, word and deed. Buddha is also regarded as a refuge because he is the re-discoverer and the exemplifier of *Dhamma* who also showed others how to live by it and experience it. He points to the faculty of wisdom developing within practitioners. He is a perfect and all-knowing unique human being who has all moral virtues, worthy of homage by gods and men (Nyunt 1999, 11-12). Thus, Buddhists bow down their heads in deep respect in front of the Buddha image.

Dhamma, the teaching of the Buddha, means truth since it enables one to see the truth. Buddhists go to the *Dhamma* for refuge because it always teaches all living beings to avoid evil, to do good merits and to purify the mind. Salvation from *samsara* is achieved by this guidance. This means that salvation in Buddhism can be obtained through following the ethical disciplines of *Dhamma*.

Lastly they go to the *Sangha* for refuge because the *Sangha* is the living stream through which the *Dhamma* flows to them. *Sangha* literally means a group or community, but here it means a group of saints or monks. Buddha substituted the *Sangha* for the family and they became the new community, virtually replacing the family in position and importance. A *bikkhu* in Pali (a monk) who sincerely follows the *Dhamma*, belongs to the *Sangha*, but he has to be celibate. Even though monks (*Sangha*) live in monasteries in reality they are the point at which the Buddha-*Dhamma* makes direct contact with humanity. In short, they are the bridge between living men and absolute truth. Thittila states the importance of *Sangha*:

> The Buddha greatly emphasized its importance as a necessary institution for the wellbeing of mankind; for, if there had not been *Sangha*, the Buddha-Dhamma would have become a mere legend and tradition after the passing of the Buddha. Not only has the *Sangha* preserved the word of the Master, but also the unique spirit of the Noble Teaching. It cannot exist, however, without the support of the lay Buddhists, *upasakas* and *upasikas*. Those who help to maintain the *Sangha*, benefit both themselves and others, for in so doing, they not only acquire merit but they are helping to keep alive and spread the Noble Teaching of Buddha, *Dhamma*. The task of each and every Buddhist is first to make the Buddha-Dhamma a living reality, by studying it and practicing it in everyday life. When we live in accordance with the *Dhamma* we can speak about it with authority. Secondly, a Buddhist's task is to spread the pure Buddha-Dhamma, or to help the Sangha, who devote their whole lives to the study, practice and spreading of the pure *Dhamma* – which is excellent in the beginning, in the middle and in the end. Thereby we become helpers of humanity and messengers of peace and happiness (2002, 209-210).

The Concept of *Kamma*, Merit and Reincarnation

The word *kamma* in Pali is equated to the action of a person, and this action also creates some karmic results, all good and bad actions (Naing 1997, 275). It is the core of Buddhism because it is the causality of *samsara*, the round of rebirth, and it determines a man's life condition. In accordance with the teaching of Buddhism, it extends the relation of cause and effect from the physical sphere to the moral sphere. Of course, every action produces an effect. But *kamma* is neither fatalism nor a doctrine of predestination. In fact, it is an impersonal, natural law that operates in accordance with our actions (Thittala 2000, 176). It is better to say that *kamma* is a law in itself and does not have any lawgiver. In the light of *kamma*, the past influences the present because man has to deserve the results of every word, thought or deed of his innumerable past lives, and the present influences the future. For these reasons, Winston L. King mentions:

> *Kamma* is the cosmic law of the inescapable reaping of the morally-deserved results of one's own deeds. Just as every physical event is the result of a preceding event or set of circumstances, and in turn acts as the cause of another event, so every deed of every sentient being produces its consequences; and the nature of those consequences is in ethical accord with the nature of the antecedent deed (1964, 129).

In accordance with its teaching, the universe resulted from *kamma* in a kind of cycle of cause and effect. Another leading Buddhist authority, Bhikkhu Buddhadasa Indapanno, equates God with impersonal *kamma*, thus rejecting God's eternal personality and his purposeful relation to his created world. Indapanno argues that if God is the cause of all things then he must be equated with *kamma* (Indapanno 1967, 66-67). Instead of the Creator God being separate from and outside of his creation, Buddhists take a monistic view that espouses *karma* and all things as parts of creation itself.

Indapanno also proposed a second view of God by equating him with *avijja* meaning lack of knowledge or ignorance. He argues that if God caused all things to exist, then he is the cause of suffering. In Buddhist views, suffering is caused by ignorance of the Four Noble Truths of the enlightened Buddha. There is no concept of God the Creator in Theravada Buddhism. Rather, creation came into being by itself. The rejection of the existence of God is a challenge to Christianity which believes that God is the pivot on which everything revolves.

Therefore, according to the teaching of Buddhism, *kamma* operates as an inescapable law of justice, independent of the decrees of God or the gods. The individual is made responsible both for his or her happiness and misery. Nothing unmerited can happen to an individual, and whatever happens, people should accept the blame for their misfortunes rather than blaming others or God. They believe that none can be saved by another, but only by his own personal effort.

The shift from the *nibbanic* to *kammatic* soteriology in turn requires a change in the concept of soteriological action. While *Nibbanic* Buddhism seeks to attain its goal through "*sila, sammadi, panna*" (what I call non-theistic ethical disciplines), *Kammatic* Buddhism aspires to achieve its goal through "work," that is, "meritorious action." It is the central ingredient in the religious experience of the Burmese people in Myanmar. In practice, "doctrinal Buddhism" is studied and known by the monks and elders, but the Buddhist lay people understand and observe the form of Buddhism that can simply be equated with merit-making. Nyunt offers this summary: "To the Burmese the essential doctrine of Buddhism is merit-making, and their interpretation of merit-making is that if a man exercises sufficient care in following the rules he need not be anxious. It depends on himself. Everyone repeats the proverbial maxim: 'In this world everything changes except good deeds and bad deeds; these follow you as the shadow follows the body'" (1999, 155-177).

According to the Burmese worldview, a person has an endless number of rebirths, and his karma covers all his prior lives including his present one. The karma of his previous and present lives will determine his future life, which he has no control over. A person's condition or disposition in any given moment is a product of his accumulated karma. On the one hand, a person's bad karma (sin) will drive him to be reborn at a lower status. On the other hand, his good karma (merit) will elevate him to be reborn at a higher status or at an advantageous position in his next life.

In theory, a person does not need to improve on his present condition since it is determined by his past karma. His present good deeds or merit are believed to be applied to the total accumulation of merit, which will then determine his position in future rebirths. Instead of improving one's present-life misfortune or suffering, a Burmese will normally emphasize the act of merit-making by giving to and offering services to a Buddhist monk or temple. By so doing, he believes that he will not have to experience the same present-life. However, Thittila points out three classification of *kamma*: "There is *kamma* that ripens in the same lifetime. *Kamma* that ripens in the next life and *kamma* that ripens in successive births. These three types of *kamma* are bound to produce results as a seed is to sprout" (2000, 180).

Even though philosophically *kamma* can direct its effects on the present life, the Burmese people, particularly in Yangon, still perceive and place a heavy emphasis on storing up good *kamma* (merit) for their next life. They seem to have another important motivation and benefit for merit-making in this present life—to transfer the merit they have acquired to their deceased family members or ancestors. This would then allow the departed ones to be reborn into a better condition. If enough merit is transferred to them, they can then be reborn in a higher position. Of course, they make merit in the hope of being reborn into a higher status or in a more favorable disposition in their next life as well as desiring to avoid being reborn as an evil spirit. This *kammic* process affects one's past, present, and future life, and it is additionally applied to all beings. In short, the cycle of rebirths, in which all existent beings are caught, is governed by the law of *kamma*.

The Nature of Sin: *Kammic* Consequences

The Buddhists deny the idea of original sin. However, sin according to Buddhism consists of three immoral actions. They are: sins committed by physical immoral actions, sins committed by vocal immoral actions and sins committed in the heart (immoral mental actions). That is why Dhammananda states that there is no such thing as sin as explained by other religions. To the Buddhists, sin is unskillful or unwholesome action—*akusala* creates the downfall of man, and the wicked man is an ignorant man. He needs instruction more than he needs punishment and condemnation. He is not regarded as violating God's will or as a person who must beg for divine mercy and forgiveness. He needs only guidance for his enlightenment (2002, 188-192). There is no being accountable to oneself and one's own *kamma,* which will affect future existences through any infractions of *sila* (precepts) or other laws. Thus, one of the fundamental ways prescribed by Buddhism for its followers to do good works is to observe the five Buddhist religious precepts for lay people. These five precepts in Pali are as follows with my English translation.

> *Panatipata veramani sikkhapadam samadhiyami*
> I undertake (to observe) the rule of abstinence from killing any living beings.
>
> *Aninnadana vermani sikkhapadam samadhiyami*
> I undertake (to observe) the rule of abstinence from stealing anything from others.
>
> *Kamesu micchacara vermani sikkhapadam samadhiyami*
> I undertake (to observe) the rule of abstinence from committing adultery.
>
> *Musavada vermani sikkhapadam samadhiyami*
> I undertake (to observe) the rule of abstinence from telling lies.
>
> *Suramerayamajjappamadatthana vermani sikkhapadam samadhiyami.*
> I undertake (to observe) the rule of abstinence from intoxicants that cause a careless frame of mind.

These precepts are intended to prevent the bad *kamma* which will definitely have consequence on one's next life and future rebirths. In reality, however, the precepts are easily broken by any Burmese who have undergone the ceremony in order to receive them. Once broken, the precepts will produce bad *kamma* which will then have future repercussions. On the other hand, observing Buddhist precepts is a preventive measure against bad *kamma* and they see the benefit of observing the precepts in a practical way. This perception can be valid that receiving the five precepts can be seen as a ritual cleansing, a purification which enables the lay people to receive the benefits of the ceremony in a proper manner.

Examining the Burmese Buddhist religious values, the vital requirement to be a Buddhist is to take refuge in the Three Gems. Comprehending the relevancy of Buddhism for the Burmese people and their concepts of *kamma*, merit, reincarnation and sin, is significant in understanding their decision-making process in daily life. When analyzing their religious values, first of all, Buddhism has a tremendous influence on the Burmese daily life decisions. Second, from the concepts of *kamma*, merit and reincarnation, the Burmese people in Yangon view present and future life as the byproduct of their total accumulation of *kamma* or good merit. These notions create a fatalistic approach to life decisions and have led the Burmese people to *kamma*-conscious and merit-oriented life philosophies. Third, they still are able to repay gratitude to their beloved dead parents and kinsmen by involving themselves with the Buddhist temples and monks. The merit gained through these merit-making activities can be transferred to help the deceased loved ones. Finally, the Burmese view sin in relation to the observance of the five precepts and in relation to the observance of the teaching of one's ancestors. The breaking of any of the five precepts and the transmission of the will of the ancestors by not conducting traditional customs, rituals, or ceremonies prescribed them is considered sinful and, therefore, automatically results in sin.

Summary

As can be seen from the discussion in terms of the socio-cultural and religious context of Burmese people, the history of Burmese people shows that they had a strong nationalistic spirit and later, from the beginning of their migration to Myanmar, their nationalism was interwoven with Buddhism. In other words, Burmese nationalism and Buddhism are identical with the Buddhist solidarity and having social and religious values in their daily life. Instead of following the tenets of Buddhism, however, they practice syncretistic Buddhism mixed with animistic practice. Being permeated with a nationalistic spirit and distinctive socio-cultural-religious values, Burmese people are reluctant to accept the gospel of Jesus Christ. In the next chapter we will see how they responded to the gospel.

CHAPTER 4

Missionaries' Communicational Approaches in Yangon City

According to Myanmar church historical records, the existence of permanent Christian communities in Myanmar has a date as early as 16th century through the European traders. Obviously these Christian communities were closely knit for their spiritual and social purposes, and for their own welfare and survival in the country. The proper history of Christianity in Myanmar, however, goes back to the appointment of two Catholic Italian priests to the Kingdom of Ava in 1720. From the scattered Catholic Christians all over the country, prior to the arrival of Protestant missionaries to Myanmar, there were two Roman Catholic churches in Yangon with about three thousand members (Purser 1913, 89). This study, however, is limited to only highlighting the traditional Protestant Christian communicational approaches of the missionary period (1813 to 1966) to the Buddhists and the present situation of churches in Yangon city.

Missionaries' Communicational Approaches (1813-1966)

The nation's political history can be divided into five periods: Monarchy (1044-1855), Colonialism (1824-1947), Parliamentary Democracy (1948-1962), the Socialist Regime (1962-1988), and Military Junta (1988 to 2010) (Myo Thant and others 2002, 8-12). Christianity in Myanmar has existed through the different phases of political change. In all these political systems the churches survived and grew year by year. In accordance with the historical record of Christianity, Protestant Christian mission entered Myanmar during the monarchical rule, but its expansion among the ethnic groups was possible after the British colonized the country. Nowadays, Christianity in Myanmar makes up 9.1% of the population, with two-thirds considered Protestant (Nyunt 2008, 104). However, a large percentage of the Christian population is found among the tribal peoples.

Since the history of Christian communication in Myanmar is vast in terms of communicational approaches this book is confined only to the Baptist missions. The rationale is that the study of Myanmar Protestant Christian history is predominantly contributed to and influenced by the Baptist missions. The largest organization, known as Myanmar Baptist Convention (MBC), has almost half of Protestant Christians in the country. It is also significant to point out some historical impacts as many younger denominations and parachurch organizations are derived from Baptist backgrounds. In addition, the approaches to communicate the gospel with people in Myanmar with all missions during the nineteenth and twentieth centuries tended to be quite similar to one another. In order to communicate the gospel to the Buddhists in Yangon during "the missionaries' period", the American Baptist missionaries used various communicational approaches such as literature ministry, *zayat* ministry, educational ministry and medical ministry.

Literature Ministry

With his arrival, the American missionary, Adoniram Judson, encountered the religious life of the country not only within the arena of Buddhism in Myanmar but also with its sacred literature (Dingrin 2006, 52-53). In view of that, to find a vehicle for the Christian message, Judson had no choice but to make himself familiar with the Burmese language. Further, he might have noticed that Burmese people had their own written language with a long tradition and the monastic educational system was a great contribution to the literacy of the Burmese people. Vuta reports:

> In order to communicate the gospel to the people, Judson began to learn Burmese, a monosyllabic and tonal language,

spoken by a majority of the people . . . Judson wrote a Burmese grammar and in January 1816, began to translate the New Testament. He also completed a tract by August of that year. He also learned Pali – the language in which the Buddhist scriptures were written (1983, 44-45).

Judson showed eagerness to do Bible translation in order to express the gospel in the vernacular culture of the Burmese. His primary purpose was none other than to see the conversion of the Burmese people (Judson 1883, 564). So there is no doubt that a series of tracts in Burmese that he wrote were also integral to his evangelistic work (Ibid., 566). For Judson "the formation of Christian literature in Myanmar indicates the meeting of the Christian gospel with Theravada Buddhism" (Dingrin 2006, 53). Christian literature was his entry point to communicate the gospel.

Having focused on a literature ministry, Judson diligently worked and spent time in distributing Christian literature to the inquirers and visitors (Wa 1963, 84-98). Consequently, many people read the pamphlets and booklets and visited the *"zayat"* (Ibid., 15, 16, 63). Probably, they wanted to learn about the messenger rather than the message or to learn more about God and the Christian religion with different attitudes. Whatever it was, seeing feedback from the recipients, Judson was convinced that the gospel needed to be communicated with the Burmese through literature. Apart from Bible translation, Judson spent about half of his time in distribution of tracts. All the literary work of Judson reflects what Sanneh calls the "translatability" of Christianity, that is, the need for translation across a cultural boundary (Sanneh 1989, 47). Thus, Judson's vernacular translation work was the re-translation of Christ into Burmese culture and language (Walls 1996, 28) and this re-translation had the potential to reshape and expand the Christian faith in Myanmar.

Zayat **Ministry**

In the Burmese religio-cultural context, *zayats* serve a different purpose from the pagodas. They give shelter and rest to the travelers and are also places where people gather to talk and share news. *Zayats* are also used by Buddhist *phongyis* (monks) on special occasions such as religious gatherings or funerals. Missiologically, the whole basis of Judson's communicational approach was person-to-person evangelism so that the inquirers could feel free to express their views as well as to hear his. In other words, it was a round-table model.

Why did Judson employ *zayat* ministry as one means of communicating the gospel with the Buddhists? Undeniably Judson encountered difficulties in communicating the gospel with Buddhists in a strange land. On the other hand, in spite of his knowledge of the Burmese language and culture, his Western philosophy of individualism still dictated the prevalence of his communication approach as preaching. His early mission strategy focused on receiving visitors in his home. As his mission station was isolated outside the community, he isolated himself from outside contact (Peam 1962, 25). These factors meant he had what L Zau Lat calls "*Mission Compound Mentality*—a self-contained kind of Christianity" (2006, 98). In view of that he did not win any convert during the first five years (1813-1818). From his failure, Judson learned the importance of a contextual lifestyle and decided to utilize this *zayat* approach in Yangon. Wa states:

> Mr Judson preached for the first time in the new *zayat* . . . , it must be regarded as an event of no ordinary importance. Here was the first altar erected in Burma for the worship of the Eternal and Everlasting God. Plain and simple as were its walls compared with the magnificent pagodas that surrounded it, [it] was perhaps the fitter emblem of that spiritual religion which delights not in temples made with hands, but in the service of the heart (1963, 15-16).

In this approach, Burmese people were not afraid to come to worship there. Judson also adapted the gospel message to the Buddhist worldview and used the Burmese language as the code of communication. As this is the lingua franca, literature written in Burmese as the medium also served to follow-up those who visited the *zayat* and wanted to study the Christian faith further. To emphasize this new approach, Francis Wayland states:

> The essence of Judson's *communication* was a combination of conviction of the truth and rationality of the Christian faith, a firm belief in the authority of the Bible, and a determination to make Christianity relevant to the Burmese mind without violating the integrity of the Christian truth, or as he put it, to *communicate* the gospel, not anti-Buddhism (1853, 126).

As Judson kept on communicating the gospel with Burmese Buddhists without anti-Buddhism, but not compromising the truth, he had so many visitors at the *zayat* that he did not even have time for study.

As a result of this method of communication, two months later Maung Naw became Judson's first convert to confess Christ in Yangon. Maung Naw's conversion had a great impact on fellow Burmese Buddhists (Vuta 1983, 46-47). By the end of August 1822, the young Burmese church grew up to eighteen members (Wa 1963, 17-25). Compared to his previous five years (1813 to 1815), within these three years (1819 to 1822), Judson had some success. The most Judson could expect from this *zayat* approach was "a web movement"—the process of people becoming Christians along with a line of families and relatives (McGavran 1970, 243). Unfortunately, from the time of U Shwe Ngong, one of the first eighteen converts, Christianity was accused before the viceroy, Mya-day-min, and consequently, visitors ceased to come to the *zayat* (Wa 1963, 12-23). The small infant church became stagnant and even a web movement hardly happened due to the resistance of society.

Educational Ministry

Judson and the American Baptist missionaries introduced missionary education in Myanmar with the help of Ma Min Lay, a Burmese Buddhist convert. In contrast with Buddhist monasteries, missionaries established two kinds of mission schools open to both boys and girls. It is noteworthy that Christian mission schools were coeducational and therefore radically different from the monastic schools which accepted boys only (Ibid., 34). From the very beginning, the gospel on the equality of the sexes in God's sight was given practical expression. Within a short while, such efforts began showing fruit, and of course, many parents began enrolling their daughters in mission schools; many boarding and high schools and even kindergartens were started in the second half of the nineteenth century (Vuta 1983, 110-111). This method through educational ministry was "not only to train local converts for ministry but to give public education to the local people regardless of race, religion and gender" (Yaw 2006, 117-118). As these schools were a great means to share the gospel with the students, the teachers tried to communicate the gospel through exerting Christian values not only on the children but on the parents as well. Accordingly, some school children were won to Christ through the school approach (Vuta 1983, 112).

The medium of these mission schools was both English and Burmese languages and along with secular subjects, the missionaries inevitably taught the Bible and Christian doctrines. However, the teaching of Christianity was later prohibited in government schools. From the missiological point of view, "Mission schools had long been an important arm of the Burma Christian church history" (Brown 1968, 12). For the higher education level, the second Protestant college was the Rangoon Baptist College founded in 1872 as middle and high school. It became a Junior College in 1901 and a degree-college in 1916, and was known as Judson College in 1920. It was developed into a university that year under the University of Calcutta. The impact of this approach was so great that these mission schools in Yangon contributed to the rising prestige of Yangon. It demonstrates that education may be one of the most appropriate means in communicating the gospel with the Burmese Buddhists. Generally speaking, almost every leader in Myanmar today is a product of Christian mission schools even though many are not Christians.

Medical Ministry

The Baptist missions suffered both persecution and natural disasters during this first period. Plagues such as cholera, dysentery, malaria, smallpox and tuberculosis were prevalent. Life expectancy was short for both the Burmese and missionaries (Wa 1963, 110-111). Due to lack of medical knowledge, indigenous people could not control the diseases, and in addition, most medical services were not really available for the masses. Because of this public health situation, missionaries felt the need to provide medical services to the people using that opportunity to communicate the gospel to the patients. Thus, the arrival on December 13, 1821 of Dr and Mrs Jonathan Price, the first medical appointees to the Burmese mission, was particularly welcome.

The first mission dispensary in Myanmar was established in 1866 in Toungoo by the American Baptist Mission, and in the first year over 4000 were treated. The American Baptist Mission established many hospitals and dispensaries around the country until the late nineteenth century. But Wa mentions that "although medical missionary work began early with the coming of Dr Jonathan Price and Dr J. Dawson, yet as compared with programs in some other countries of Asia and Africa, it would seem that medical work has had comparatively little emphasis in Burma" (Ibid., 38). For instance, in Yangon, and with the sponsorship of the Woman's American Baptist Foreign Mission Society, Mrs M. C. Douglass opened a hospital department at Kyimyindine mission building in 1882. It proved to be a very worthwhile effort. Since a large number of people, female and male, adults and children, were attached to the hospital, it helped the missionaries to establish a good rapport with the local communities. Encouraged by the results, in 1887 the missionaries opened a woman's hospital and nurses' training school on Mission Road, now known as *Duffering* Hospital in Yangon (Ibid., 244-245). This woman's hospital was helpful to women in giving treatment at low cost and it continued as the largest government maternity hospital in the country till late nineteenth century, though very few people know of its Christian beginnings. On the other hand, patients felt the compassion of nurses and doctors and had the opportunity to hear and experience the love of God while in the hospital. Even today, it is the best women's hospital in the whole country.

In addition, Miss Marian Shivers also started the Baptist Spectacles Clinic and even a few local staff were involved. Then, a Christian hospital was run by the local Christian community of Anglican, Baptist, and Methodist churches as a home mission project. Myanmar Christian doctors and nurses were given a larger share in its management which promised wider usefulness and increased medical efficiency (Ibid., 245).

These medical ministries, such as assisting women in delivering babies and general care at *Duffering* hospital, assisting the needy people at the

Optical clinic, and a Christian hospital, offered good opportunities for the Christian missionaries to communicate the gospel. Such ministries were much appreciated, since they met a long-standing need. Medical ministries yielded some fruit in terms of conversions even though missionaries encountered hardship, but the results were far from satisfactory for the missionaries with only a few converts from Burmese Buddhist backgrounds. The missionaries not only saved the souls but they also healed the physical body.

The Judsons and other American missionaries employed appropriate methods to communicate the gospel with Burmese Buddhists in Yangon. However, due to the incompatible concepts of the gospel message and the Buddhist philosophy, and the total domination of their social, political and spiritual life by Buddhism, the Burmese Buddhists could not appreciate the gospel from the very beginning, as Buddhism fills the mind, grips the emotions, and directs the life in certain very definite forms of conduct.

Examining Missionaries' Communicational Approaches

Lack of Credibility of the Communicator Principle

After Judson's era in 1852, there were only 267 Burmese Buddhist converts and even today it represents slow growth with about 0.1% of the Christian population in the country. If we search deeply through the early accounts of church history and examine it from the different perspectives, we may come across reasons why Burmese people treated the missionaries so badly when it was they who had brought the light of the world to Myanmar.

The Burmese people viewed American Baptist missionaries as parts of Colonialism rather than religious teachers. Burmese historians, when they were thoroughly analyzing Burmese history, discovered Judson's letter to Colonel Benson dated 18 July 1838, in which he said that "to be successful in Christian mission among the Burmese people . . . to occupy their country is the best way" (Thein Han 2003, 223). Burmese researchers also had a chance to study Colonel Benson's letter to the Governor-General. "This gentleman (Dr Judson) avows himself predisposed for war, as the best, if not the only means of eventually introducing the humanizing influences of the Christian religion" (Trager 1966, xi). Maung Htin Aung who had been Vice-Chancellor of the University of Yangon and Chairman of the Myanmar Historical Commission, firmly believed that American missionaries had been involved in the British occupation of Myanmar. "A distressing aspect of this continuing campaign against the Burmese was the fact that the American missionaries took part in it" (Ibid., xi). How were American missionaries involved in the British Imperialistic movement? Nyunt states:

> The missionaries were not neutral; they welcomed the British. Instead of being anxious or fearful about the prospects of a war, the Americans regarded the invading British army as a friendly, liberating force. For the Americans, the identification of the "English" with the "Christian" made them blurred the distinction between "vocational" and "political" considerations and concerns. Finally, the missionaries welcomed the British, above all else, because they believed that through the instrumentality of a British conquest, Christianity could be propagated freely in Burma. To the Burmese, as they were aware and suspicious of the missionaries' attitude and movements, they treated them as they had the European betrayal (Portugal, French . . .) and as potential enemies. . . . The American missionaries in their writings presented a monstrous picture of the people to whose country they had come uninvited. It seems that, to the Burmese nationalist eyes, both (the Americans and the British India Company) desired the same end, namely the speedy conquest of the Burmese kingdom by the British (2006, 118-119).

The Burmese people suspected Judson was pro-British as he did take part in the political situation. He served as a negotiator and interpreter when the British and Burmese made the Treaty of Peace at *Yandabo* on February 24, 1826, after the first War between them (Trager 1966, 23). At that time, the Burmese king requested Judson to remain at Ava by promising him honors and rewards, and granting religious toleration. However, Judson agreed to accompany the English civil commissioner, Mr Crawford, "to assist in the selection of the site of the new capital for the provinces ceded to the British." The Judson family moved there as soon as they got a place (Ibid., 27).

Nevertheless, in 1828, Judson examined himself and realized that he should stop his affiliation with the British officers if he was truly to follow Jesus. He gave up all social engagements with British society and refused to receive an honorary doctorate degree which had been given him. He also wrote to his family in America to destroy all his letters (Wa 1963, 75). Although Judson changed his attitude, the British invaders and some American missionaries were still inseparable from the British to the Burmese eyes. Their imperialistic approach stimulated the Burmese nationalistic attitude. Smith quoted from King Thibaw's proclamation issued before the 3rd Anglo-Burmese War in 1886, mentions:

> To the headmen of all towns and villages . . . And all subjects and inhabitants of the royal territories: Those heretics, the English barbarians, having most harshly made demands likely to impair and destroy our religion, violate our national customs and degrade our race, are making a display and preparation as if about to wage war against our state . . . if these heretic barbarians should come and attempt to molest or disturb the state in any way, His Majesty the King, watchful that the interests of religion and of the state shall not suffer, will himself march forth . . . and will gain for us the notable result of placing us in the path to the celestial regions and to Nirvana, the eternal rest (1965, 84).

Consequently, the concept that the missionaries used Christianity as a tool to occupy the country caused a lack of credibility of Christian mission, which is still deeply rooted in Burmese minds till today.

Lack of Frame of Reference Principle

According to this principle, communication is most effective when the communicator, his message and the receptor are part of a common frame of reference. As mentioned earlier, Burmese people have a nationalistic spirit and always pride themselves on being Buddhists; they never feel themselves inferior to any people of other faiths nor do they intend to subordinate their Buddhist faith to any foreign faith. Therefore, there was no other way for the missionaries to choose to present the gospel message in terms of the Burmese frame of reference. Employing this principle requires that the communicator (missionary) understands the frame of reference of the Burmese people and starts where they are. But what Judson did as an opponent can be seen in his tract, "The Golden Balance".

In "The Golden Balance" (Howard 1931, 211-124), Judson designated only his own frame of reference. For instance, Judson preached in comparison and in contrast to the Burmese Buddhist beliefs. The whole content of "The Golden Balance" reflects how much better the religion preached by Judson was than the religion encountered locally. Throughout the tract, Judson made attempts to compare the eternal God, Christ and Christianity with Gautama the Buddha and Buddhism; the Christian Scripture and the Buddhist Tripitaka; the Christian priests and the Buddhist monks. More often, Judson used comparative terms like "truer" or "more excellent" to show the superiority of Christianity over Burmese Buddhism. Also, he exclusively regarded the Christian God or Christ as the right and more excellent one; Christian priests or teachers as more excellent; Christianity as the truer religion; Christian Scripture more reliable than the *Tripitaka*; the law of Gautama the Buddha as defective with a punishing system which cannot really remove the root of sin; and the law of Christ as a pardoning system, which can effectively strike at the root of sin, fulfilling the requirements of all other commandments. The call to the Burmese Buddhist to choose the true God, the excellent one and the true religion is the main theme of the tract (Wayland 1953, 448-458). Hence based on the weak spiritual potential he found in Buddhism and the moral deficiencies he experienced through the lives of the Burmese Buddhists, Judson (and his fellow missionaries) concluded that Burmese Buddhism was lacking in the transforming power that can create a new spirituality in the lives of its adherents.

The Catholic missionaries also pointed out the void of spiritual vigor in the teaching system of Burmese Buddhism and moral deficiencies in the daily lives of the Buddhist monks and laymen. For instance, Father Vincentius Sangermano, one of the earliest Catholic missionaries wrote, "The Law of Guatama teaches not to kill any living things, yet fishermen are encouraged for the sake of the *ngapi* (fish paste) . . . the Law of Guatama forbids polygamy, but still the Burmese people, besides their lawful wife, have two or three concubines" (Vincentius Sangermano 1883, 159, 164). Hence, such negative and "better-than-thou" attitudes have shaped the Myanmar Christian thinking and gradually led them to see Buddhism and other religions as inferior to Christianity. That is why Pe Maung Tin wrote, "The missionaries evidently came to teach, neither to learn nor to make Buddhists the object of their missionary love and concern. Rather, the Buddhists are seen only as the object of their missionaries preaching" (1961, 28). Such missionary attitudes and prejudice seem to be one of the facts that hindered the work of Adoniram Judson so that he took about six years to win a devout Burmese Buddhist, Maung Naw.

Furthermore, both missionaries and early Christians in Myanmar had often preached the gospel with the wrong view that Christianity far outweighed Buddhism and all other religions, and hence with this view disdainfully looked down upon the Buddhists and people of other faiths as inferior and a bunch of hell-bound people. These one-sided and exclusive attitudes made the Christian gospel unattractive to the Buddhists in Myanmar.

Lack of Contextualization

I learned to open up to Burmese culture, their social and religious values and relationships, as well as using the principles and methods Christians have used in communicating the gospel. Christian missionaries in Myanmar did not seem to be so active in indigenizing the gospel and in adapting themselves to the Burmese context. Rather, Christianity in Myanmar seems Westernized, generally regarded as a foreign religion. Its instructions are foreign. The architecture of its buildings is foreign. Its music is foreign. Its emphasis on individual conversion and separation of its members from their original social relationships also cause people to regard it as foreign.

All foreignness constitutes a difficult barrier for the present-day missionary to overcome. Above all, this lack of contextuality fails to consider the relevance of the message to the needs of the receptor.

According to *Nibbanic* Buddhism, the ultimate need of Buddhists is enlightenment or obtaining *nibbana*, not a perpetuation of reincarnation. But Judson used in his Bible translation the words "eternal life or heaven" as the result for those who believe in God. Ironically for the Buddhists, eternal life could mean the biggest curse they can think of. "It is understood in terms of a predestined process, a miserable cyclic rise and fall of one meaningless, aimless reincarnation after another" (Davis 1993, viii). It means an eternal perpetuation of their meaningless existence caused by the understanding of the law of *kamma* and its consequent hells and rebirths. I also used this term in preaching the gospel to Burmese Buddhists. In 1995 I started a church among the Burmese Buddhist community and in January 1996 I baptized one Burmese Buddhist convert. Later, he became a backslider. After his water baptism, I used to teach him the Word of God. One day, he told me that Jesus could not liberate him from the circle of *samsara* or circle of rebirth even though he changed his religion. The reason was that Jesus could promise him only eternal life. That means that Jesus causes him to remain bound in *samsara*. So it was better for him to be a Buddhist again. I was shocked hearing him. I realize how a Buddhist understands the concept of eternal life.

According to Buddhist terminology, heaven is part of "thirty-existence" and interchangeably used with one of twenty Brahma planes (see the diagram of Jesus as liberator from *samsara*). Buddhists believe that those who have acquired lots of merits are to be reborn in heaven when they pass away. In addition, heaven is a place of extreme happiness. However, according to their beliefs, those in heaven are still subject to the law of *kamma* and the cycle of rebirth as much as those on earth and in hell. So this lack of contextuality in communicating the final goal of believing in Christ is poles apart from the relevancy of Buddhist belief.

The foreign missionaries described the Burmese people's need to hear the gospel. However, they failed to consider the receptor-oriented communicational questions: who are the receptors?, where are the receptors?, what are their needs and how to meet their needs? It would have been more effective communication if they had focused on receptor-oriented communication. Ironically, their communication was not receptor-oriented. Also they did not understand the socially-oriented Burmese people but preached the gospel to the individual.

The National Christian Church (1966 to Present)

Since the time of the American missionaries, a harvest was reaped mainly from mission fields in the remote areas of the country among the indigenous hill tribes. People were more open to the gospel there and willing to change their religion and become literate. With great efforts, the Baptist mission in Myanmar had converted almost all the animist tribal groups of Myanmar. Some of these groups became Christians almost hundred percent; for instance the Kachin and Chin tribal groups were over 90%. The church has grown particularly well among the Kayin, Chin and Kachin tribal groups; however, the growth among the Burmese still remains stagnant.

Due to the declaration of Buddhism as the state religion by Prime Minister U Nu, the revival of Buddhism became an important part of state activity. In view of the issue of the state religion during the democratic government in Myanmar (1948-1962) it became more difficult for Christians to propagate the gospel in the country (Win, Han, and Hlaing 1991, 14, 92).

In 1962 the Myanmar Armed Forces under the leadership of General Ne Win seized power and set up the Revolutionary Council and of course, the rule of U Nu's Parliamentary Democracy came to an end. The Council established a military dictatorship and began to develop Socialist rule over the country. Then they published the statement of their ideology, "the Burmese Way to Socialism", in April 1962. In 1974, the Revolutionary Council transferred its power to the Socialist Government (Smith 1965, 26). The main characteristics of the Socialist government were based on Buddhist beliefs. Its motto was "man matters most," a conglomeration of Buddhism and Marxism. Its main teaching was "the middle way" based on Buddhist philosophy.

The act of the Revolutionary Council had a great impact on Christianity. In 1962-1964, the Socialist Government expelled all missionaries, devalued people's money, and nationalized all Christian Mission Schools and Mission Hospitals and Dispensaries and other non-religious institutions like farms, orphanages' etc. In such a situation the church in Myanmar was like sheep without shepherds. It was the end of the missionaries' period in the history of the Myanmar church and a new page opened for the national Christian leaders to carry on mission. Zau Lat states:

> In the post-missionary period, under the former Socialist Military Government, beginning with the 1960s, the churches became limited both in resources and trained personnel to engage in active mission work among non-Christians. The churches at that time were busy fighting for their own 'survival,' for they had suddenly become independent autonomous churches from being "mission fields" of the American churches . . . There were very few mission works the churches could do outside of the church compounds. Christians were free to worship inside the church building at all times, but it was hard to get permission to hold big gatherings like Annual Meetings of Convention. The churches have no more access to their once most effective arms of evangelization: the mission schools, hospitals, and mission farms. Once again all church activities were confined to the church compounds and thus, Christians in Myanmar began to develop a form of "*Mission Compound Mentality*," establishing "*self-contained kind of churches,*" very rapidly, thereby sharing the good news of the Lord only in the churches, among its members, and thus limiting their mission work, *in the world* (2006, 86-87).

Lat does not mean that the church in Myanmar became stagnant after the missionary period, but he emphasizes that the churches had to face hardship leading the flocks in the "valley of the shadow of death" under the Marxist-oriented military government of Myanma Socialist Lanzin, that is, the Myanmar Socialist Program Party which was then waging a war fiercely against autonomous states.

Due to the economic crisis, general demonstrations for democracy and riots against the Socialist Government broke out in the whole country. After the 1988 incident, the ruling power of the country was passed on to the younger generation of generals by the senior military Junta. As the people demanded a change, the military Junta liberated the economy and opened up the "closed door" of the country a little bit. Taking advantage of the situation, many Christian groups who wanted to "plant churches" in this country of "the land of golden pagodas," came in different ways as businessmen, language teachers, and workers in NGOs. With the help of national Christian churches, foreign missionaries made great efforts to plant new churches in accordance with their own understanding of the Bible and their ways of worship. However, the sad thing today is that mission work among the Burmese Buddhists is still 'hitting against a thick brick wall and thus it is in a big crisis.'

Tracing the approaches of the national churches from U Nu to Than Shwe periods, the church in Yangon has increased to some extent representing about four percent of the city population (Yangon Christian Directory 2005, 50). It seems to be sizable but still is only a fraction of the city's population. The Burmese Christians are only a handful whereas the majority of the city's population is Buddhist. The churches in Yangon enjoy relative freedom of worship but have been employing the missionaries' methods without any critical evaluation.

Summary

Roman Catholics first introduced Christianity. Protestant mission expanded through the arrival of the American Baptist mission. The first phase of mission totally focused on the Burmese Buddhists particularly in Yangon through a variety of approaches by the American Baptist missionaries, the Judsons, and other commendable ones. Judson gathered together a group of Burmese Buddhist converts as the first Protestant church in Yangon after many trials. When missionaries left the country by 1966, there was a very small number of Burmese Christians. As to the cause, there might be different answers on this issue. One undeniable fact is that the Burmese are community-oriented people and when they become converts, they have to give up long-held beliefs and social attachments such as family, friends and community. Not being able to mix with their friends and having to form a separate community causes a lot of inconvenience. From the outset, the missionaries discouraged the faithful converts from walking, standing and sitting with non-Christians. The missionaries' goal in this was to prevent the new converts from backsliding, but it led to the adverse result of the Christians becoming an isolated and distinct community. This isolation and separation of the Christian community from the Burmese Buddhists finally becomes a great barrier in communicating the gospel.

CHAPTER 5

Contemporary Christian Communication in Yangon City

The following analysis is a summary of personal interviews with twenty Protestant Christian leaders and a questionnaire to 111 Burmese Buddhist converts living in Yangon. Both instruments had been tested beforehand. Their answers can help in developing more contextual ways of Christian communication for the contemporary Burmese Buddhist context.

Results of the Interviews

From the large number of Protestant churches in Yangon, only twenty Christian leaders were selected who live in Yangon and have been in ministries for more than ten years. From the sample populations, seventeen were male and three female. These twenty respondents comprised the sample population for the interviews. These respondents were selected from the following categories of ministerial experiences: local church pastors, denominational and organizational leaders and Bible school teachers. According to these categories of respondents' leadership responsibilities, a pattern was identified. There were ten (50%) in pastoral leadership, six (30%) in denominational/organizational leadership, and four (20%) in theological education (teaching in Bible school). The insights gained from them allowed viewing potential differences of perception and experiences in Christian communication among the Buddhist Burmese society. Thus, the results of the survey were not the observations of outside observers, but

TABLE 1: Demographic Information of Respondents

Respondents	Age	Years in Ministry	Office	Affiliation
RP1	56	13	Local Pastor	Baptist
RP2	53	20+	Local Pastor	Anglican
RP3	48	12	Local Pastor	Baptist
RP4	70+	30+	Local Pastor	Brethren
RP5	50+	19	Local Pastor	Methodist
RP6	40	18	Local Pastor	Assembly of God
RP7	53	14	Local Pastor	Evangelical Free Church
RP8	50+	17	Local Pastor	Assembly of God
RP9	51	16	Local Pastor	Church of Christ
RP10	49	16	Local Pastor	Independent
RD1	65+	20+	Denomination Leader	Baptist
RD2	55	20+	Denomination Leader	Methodist
RD3	65+	30+	Denomination Leader	Assembly of God
RD4	58	25+	Denomination Leader	United Pentecostal Church
RD5	50+	15+	Denomination Leader	Bread of Life
RD6	60+	25+	Organization Leader	Para-Church
RT1	39	12	Bible School Teacher	Assembly of God
RT2	46	12	Bible School Teacher	Baptist
RT3	45+	15	Bible School Teacher	Full Gospel
RT4	54	17	Bible School Teacher	Church of God

the self-understanding of those who were themselves involved in Christian communication. In order to respect the privacy and confidentiality, interviews were coded in the following manner. The word "respondent" is abbreviated as R. The second character refers to "P" for pastor, "D" for denominational/organizational leader and "T" for Bible school teacher. The number that follows is a code number one through twenty. For example, RP1 refers to pastor one and RD5 denominational or organization leader five and RT2 Bible is school teacher two. Of the twenty respondents, thirteen were persons with whom I had previous contact or who were my acquaintances. All were in prominent positions of Christian leadership. The second way respondents were selected was through contact with a third party. The thirteen original respondents were asked to recommend others who would be eligible and willing to be interviewed. So this research technique was based on "snowball sampling" (see Babbie 2004, 148).

The interviews were carried out through a qualitative approach for interview using goal-directed conversation which interacts "between an interviewer and a respondent in which the interviewer has a general plan of inquiry" (Ibid.,300). I used the "method of constant comparison and contrast," which is said to be very practical and effective for analysis. This method provided a clear series of steps, which could help me to manage the large amount and complex nature of qualitative data more easily by comparing codes to find consistencies and differences in the patterns and themes.

Through the interviews more detailed information was obtained about the contemporary perspective of Christian communication to Burmese Buddhists. Reviewing the interviews I discovered that several major themes were explored: goals for communication, communication approaches, communication methods and media in communication, problems and challenges in communication, and contextual factors for the acceptance of the gospel by Burmese Buddhists.

When we look at the size and composition of the population in fourteen churches, we notice that while the Baptist and Assemblies of God represent 40% of the respondents, the other 60% were from twelve different churches. The rationale of selection was that these two organizations represent the majority of Protestant Christianity in the country, and in Yangon they are doing missions among the Burmese people more than other churches.

Goals for Communication

As mentioned earlier, the results of the survey are only the perspectives of the respondents being interviewed. Respondents who were asked for their perception of Christian communication had clear goals, which they knew and could explain. Two goals clearly emerged. For the vast majority of the respondents, an important goal was to convert the Burmese Buddhists through the credibility of the communicator and to avoid extracting the converts from their community and to help them to maintain close relations with their family. As mentioned in chapter 1, the credibility of the communicator plays an important role. For the converts, only if their lives were in danger would they be removed from their family, and in that case they would be encouraged and helped to re-establish close relations with their family and community. Otherwise, they should remain with the family. "I think that we need to think of the importance of the communicator in communicating the gospel with our friends who are Burmese Buddhists as they accept the messenger before they accept the message. Moreover, we should not separate the converts from the family so that they can demonstrate Christ through their transformed lives within the family and even community," stated RP2.

The other goal that emerged involved the question of the incorporation of Burmese Buddhist converts into existing churches. Only a few respondents gave high priority to the development of a community of Burmese Christians rather than to individual conversion. Ideally speaking, "evangelizing the Burmese Buddhists aims to share the gospel with them and to commence a new church with converts" claimed RT2. This means that for the vast majority of the respondents, the conversion of individuals was seen as the goal of the mission work. In the light of this, it is not surprising that a few respondents distanced themselves from the traditional goal of integrating Burmese Buddhist converts into existing congregations, whereas one major trend indicated that their mission aimed at integrating converts into existing non-Burmese congregations. The vast majority of the respondents indicated that their gospel communication aimed at integrating converts into existing non-Burmese congregations, and in fact there are no Burmese congregations in Yangon, and this could explain the very low priority of the development of Burmese Christian congregations. Furthermore, most of the respondents felt that it was not the goal of Christian communication to establish such congregations.

The information gained about the development of a Burmese Christian community and the incorporation of Burmese Christians into existing non-Burmese congregations forms a coherent pattern. To summarize these data in general, the Protestant churches in Yangon were zealous in reaching the Burmese Buddhists with the gospel to some extent but did not give high priority to the creation of communities of Burmese Christians. On the contrary they tended to focus on converting individual Burmese and then integrating them into existing non-Burmese congregations under the Christian leaders from minority ethnic groups.

Communication Approaches

We will now consider to what extent the communication approaches are contextual. As stated in chapter 1, contextualization involves faithfulness to the Bible and an attempt to relate it meaningfully to the context. The responses from the interviewees stated that faithfulness to the Bible was the most important mission principle. Most respondents gave the highest priority to the authority of the Bible. When it comes to taking the Burmese context seriously in the development of communication approaches, however, the churches appeared to be more reluctant.

Most of the respondents stated that they used culturally relevant approaches with which the Burmese were familiar. "Evangelism and social service are inseparable in church evangelistic missions," said RP5 and RT1. For these respondents, social service comes first followed by evangelism. On the other hand, a minority of the respondents stated that communication approaches should not be confused with social service. It should be pure evangelistic communication, otherwise, we will not see the result as much as we expect. "To my observation, most Burmese converts become backsliders when they do not get any benefits from their change of religion due to starting our evangelistic approach together with social service. This does not mean that social service is unimportant but gospel should come first, and service should follow if necessary," expressed RD2.

The above findings reflect the fact that most Protestant churches in Yangon were not only involved in preaching the gospel, but also in a variety of social services. By and large, the mission of the Protestant churches in Yangon was need-oriented, and of course, the approach focused on meeting specific needs of their receptors. However, it may be that not all of their holistic activities took seriously the actual needs of these Burmese Buddhists.

The most remarkable finding was that churches use the same approach in reaching Burmese Buddhists as is used in reaching other ethnic groups. Evidently, "when we initiated social service with our local churches, the door opened to us to do evangelistic works more than before. We also practice it here in Yangon in reaching the Buddhists as well," said RD4 proudly. Another comment appeared from RP7 that social service greatly contributed to reach our Buddhist friends with the gospel. "It is relevant and helpful to them wherever we initiate our missions in our country as many people are suffering from economic crisis." These findings illustrate that the Protestant churches' mission work among the Burmese people in Yangon is fairly traditional. They are following what missionaries did without any critical evaluation. Despite their good intentions for taking seriously the context of the Burmese, the communication approaches of churches were largely geared to the needs of the Burmese and adapted to their cultural patterns. The conclusion is that traditional approaches to mission are still very influential in their ministries. Also, in spite of their attitudes regarding relations to the Burmese converts to their community, the traditional policy of integrating converts into non-Burmese congregations still predominates.

All respondents agreed that their churches used a person-based approach with emphasis on personal testimony and the life of Christian ministers. There seemed to be a realization that this approach was very important for reaching the Burmese Buddhists. Taking into consideration the present situation of the churches in Yangon, churches are following their own mission principles without cooperating with neighboring churches. It shows churches in Yangon are very denominational or traditional.

Communication Methods and Media

Dayton and Fraser state that, "methods in evangelism are important even if they are not sufficient to guarantee desired results. *So any communication process* (italics mine) that takes the gospel seriously must take the methods of communicating it seriously" (Dayton and Fraser 1990, 174). The purpose of this portion of the survey was to discover which methods and media the Protestant churches in Yangon used in reaching the Burmese Buddhists. The methods may be universal, but the application is contextual. Asked specifically about the significance of methods, most respondents stated that personal witnessing was most appropriately used, whereas a few mentioned distributing gospel tracts followed by personal witness. "Our government does not distinguish religious and political issues. All the time they mix these two in one like a coin with two faces. So if we would like to evangelize our Buddhist friends, it is better to find a way to initiate conversation in our present context and lead them to the gospel later," expressed RP3. On the other hand, RT2 mentioned that, "prior to our witness about Jesus, if our Buddhist friends can read any information that we want to talk to them about, it is easier than blindly sharing the gospel with them." There seemed to be a realization of the dominant trend that a person-based approach was most important in the awareness phase for reaching the Buddhists in Yangon.

In fact, the media of communication are extensions of personal, direct, oral communication over time and space to larger audiences. There are communicational situations where media is available to use. In accordance with the present situation in Yangon, most of the respondents mentioned that the Bible or Christian literature were the main media. "Bible is our guide to communicate the gospel to Buddhists. For instance, if we do not refer to the Bible, our neighboring Buddhists may not seriously consider the message we communicate with them. If we use other media like books and cassette tapes with comparison between Christianity and Buddhism, it is very dangerous," said RD1. Significantly, RP10 expressed the belief based on his ministerial experiences among Buddhists that introducing the basic teachings of Buddhism to our Buddhist friends was the best way in sharing the gospel. But in fact, the majority of the respondents stated the Buddhist scripture was not really of any use in their communication activities. There seems to be a great reluctance among Christian churches in Yangon to use the Buddhist scripture in their ministry. Rather, the Bible is predominantly used in all phases (awareness, conversion and incorporation) of communication among the Protestant churches in Yangon.

Further, it reveals the lack of a frame of reference in Protestant church communication; this causes great problems in contextualizing the gospel among Burmese Buddhists.

Problems and Challenges

It seems obvious that the failure of missions to make a significant impact in communicating with the Burmese Buddhists is still due to both Buddhist barriers and missiological weaknesses. When asked about the problems encountered in communicating the gospel to the Burmese, two issues appeared. First was the problem of the social solidarity of Buddhism. Then there were theological barriers in expressing the doctrine of God; forgiveness of sin in particular. "Most Buddhists whom I share the gospel with seldom refuse to listen, but to accept Christ as their personal Savior is unthinkable for them. They said, "We are Burmese Buddhists," expressed RP4. It seems their indoctrination in the typical philosophy of "to be Burmese is to be Buddhist" is a great barrier in the communication process. On the other hand, the gospel message needs to be clearly communicated so that the realization of the distinction between social solidarity and spirituality would make sense. Another respondent |RP8 expressed that, "when I tell my Buddhist neighbor that everyone is sinner and salvation is obtained through the forgiveness of sin by the works of Jesus Christ on the cross, he said that it is for Christians not for Buddhists." It is obvious that theological terms in Buddhism and Christianity have different meanings. These findings show that receptor-oriented communication was neglected and communicator-orientation was favored. Because the communicator did not communicate their message within a frame of reference of the receptors, it seemed that communication was one-way.

Secondly, there was the issue of contextualization in the Burmese cultural context. The vast majority of the respondents stated that evangelism revolves around the problem of meaning, especially in cultures saturated with Buddhism. "Whenever I share the gospel with my Burmese friends, I truly want them to understand and accept the gospel. But usually they respond, 'All religions are good,'" expressed RP4. RT3 stated that, "effective communication totally depends on how we make the message easily understood by our Buddhist friends." This finding shows the Protestant churches need to appropriately contextualize the gospel message in order to be understandable for the receptors. This approach with contextualization of the message, however, must be grounded in Scripture.

When asked about the challenges some Buddhists had to face in following Jesus Christ, almost all the respondents said that they were afraid of ex-communication from their family, the loss of their job and ignorance of their friends. "One of my friends is willing to follow Jesus but till now he is still hesitant because of his family pressure," said RP7. But RP5 and RP2 said, "Burmese Buddhists worry about losing their Burmese identity and even all social ties if they become Christians." Both these findings seem to reflect that most churches are still following the traditional ways of what missionaries did previously. That is, when there is a new convert, instead of helping them to maintain close relations with family and community, they try to separate the convert from them. This seems to be contradicting their goal of communication.

The Contributive Factors to accepting the Gospel

The Burmese Buddhists seldom immediately accept the gospel as soon as they hear it. It is an affirmed fact that communication is a process. Asked about the contributing factors, several issues appeared from the respondents depending on their ministerial experiences. To summarize these issues, when their Buddhist friends see the genuine concern of churches through words and deeds of their personal witness, they decide to follow Jesus, pointed out RP5. But most respondents perceived that when Burmese Buddhists truly realized that their good works, which are grounded in religion, could not guarantee their salvation, they decided to follow Jesus. These findings reflect that the churches need to communicate the gospel integrating words and deeds; non-theistic ethical disciplines and faith in Christ are quite different in terms of salvation.

Summary and Conclusion

Based on the interviews, it seems that Christian churches in Yangon theoretically understand that gospel communicational approaches to Burmese people should be different from traditional missions among most other ethnic groups. The fact is that these Burmese people dominate the society with Buddhist philosophy, which is all pervasive, permeating the concepts and worldviews of a people and saturating their culture, language, education, and attitudes with Buddhistic viewpoints. It distinguishes them radically from most of the other ethnic groups, and calls for new communicational principles and approaches. Practically, however, churches are still following traditional approaches without any critical evaluation.

Implicitly the vast majority of churches in Yangon have been oriented to reach the Burmese people with the gospel to some extent. But unfortunately, there has been no cooperation between churches to reach this Burmese society. Rather, they focus on their agenda of church activities. In other words, they are in their linear ministry. This survey shows that the realization of the need for incorporation in Burmese missions has not yet penetrated the Protestant churches in Yangon.

According to information gained from the respondents, there is a lack of contextualization in communicating the gospel with Burmese Buddhists. Significantly, most respondents were still not ready to exchange traditional approaches with more culturally relevant and contextually appropriate approaches. In the area of language, all communicators strongly emphasized using Burmese language but still many of them were not yet familiar with Buddhist terms. In general, most churches were hesitant to make use of the Buddhist scripture. This may be a sign of their negative attitudes towards Buddhist religion and its scriptures.

From the interviews it appeared that churches from different denominations perceived that the community had to be taken seriously in missions to Burmese people. This survey, however, shows that despite their goal of communication intending the converts to stay with their family, they still largely followed the principle of individual conversion in such a way that all converts were effectively separated from their family. After converts are separated from their family, the churches attempted to re-establish the convert's relationship with their own family. At the same time, they are following the traditional approach of the Burmese Buddhist converts being integrated into existing congregations. The fact is that at the time of the interview there were still no Burmese congregations in Yangon. The conclusion, therefore, is that the mission of churches among the Burmese people in Yangon to a large extent follows traditional mission principles.

Analysis of the Results from the Survey of Burmese Buddhist Converts

In the previous section, the focus was the mission principles the churches in Yangon followed and the approaches and methods they had employed in communicating the gospel to the Burmese Buddhists. In this section, we look at the communication process from the perspective of the Burmese people who have received the gospel. I will analyze the missions of churches among the Burmese people by identifying the communicational and contextual factors that have impacted their spiritual journey. First, I will attempt to describe, in terms of their demographic characteristics, the group of Burmese people who have become Christians in the Protestant churches. Then I will determine the impact of mission initiatives, contextual factors to communicate the gospel to the Burmese society in each of the three phases of their spiritual journey (awareness phase, conversion phase, and incorporation phase). Finally, I will analyze their response to the gospel in terms of their spiritual maturity and their new relationship with the Christian community and the Burmese community. The following analysis is based on responses from 111 Burmese Christians to the questionnaire.

The questionnaire was divided into three sections. The first had six questions dealing with demographic data and the second section with time of conversion. The last section dealt with different factors which had influenced their spiritual journey in each of the three phases of their conversion process. To undertake this field research, one hundred and thirty forms were distributed in four districts of Yangon Municipal Area. Of these forms, 111 were completed and returned. The following analysis was based on their responses.

Demographic Information

The following table lists the demographic details of the sample 111 Burmese Buddhist converts who responded to the questionnaires.

TABLE 2: Demographic Information of 111 Burmese Buddhist Converts

		No	Percentage
Gender	Male	65	59%
	Female	46	41%
Age	Below 20	10	9%
	Between 20 and 29	30	27%
	Between 30 and 39	35	32%
	Between 40 and 49	25	22%
	50+ . . .	11	10%
Marital Status	Single	35	32%
	Married	76	68%
Education	Primary School	15	14%
	Middle School	17	15%
	High School	40	36%
	College/University	20	18%
	Others	19	17%
Occupation	Christian Ministers	5	4%
	Government Servants	20	18%
	Company Employees	15	14%
	Unemployed	32	29%
	Others	39	35%
Length of Stay in Yangon	1-3 Years	12	11%
	4-6 Years	15	13%
	7-10 Years	13	12%
	11-15 Years	23	21%
	Born in Yangon	48	43%

The Communicators and the Media Channels

In my original dissertation, as an academic exercise I had a detailed analysis of data information. However, in this section I summarize data analysis to make it more accessible for a wider readership. Based on the analysis of data information through the questionnaire to 111 Burmese Buddhist converts, one of the clearest conclusions is that, in the perception of the Burmese converts, their personal interactions with Christians, with individuals or the church fellowship impacted their spiritual journey the most. The data gives the strong impression that the life of Christians and the fellowship of Christians with the Burmese people were the main channels for the message. Ideally speaking, the most important type of person had been the Christian minister. For most of the Burmese people, the actual presence of a church in the neighborhood was significant, but even more significant was the worship and fellowship in the churches, where the Burmese people apparently felt welcomed and at ease.

In the analysis of the activities of the churches or the mission of the churches, it was found that the principles of a "person-based approach with a focus on personal testimony and the life of Christian ministers" were given high priority. However, churches were not in cooperation, rather they were following their own agenda in mission work. The insufficient cooperation between the denominations in terms of missions of the churches and the local congregations may be the reason a significant percentage of the Burmese Buddhist converts complained that the Christians did not welcome them in the church during the decision and incorporation phases.

The thing most appreciated by the Burmese Buddhist converts were the personal communication channels, including prayer and personal witness. In the missional activities of the churches, social services were seen as a very important way of communicating the gospel. The Burmese people, however, did not see such activities as having much influence on their spiritual journey although these probably had an indirect influence by bringing the Burmese Buddhists into contact with Christians in medical treatments and other programs. The Burmese people may not have perceived the social services to have impacted their spiritual journey, but there are good reasons to believe that communicators through social services established personal contacts with Burmese people that later came to play a significant role in their conversion into the Christian faith. Concerning media the Burmese people often perceived such approaches to be less significant. Throughout all conversion phases, the missions of the churches gave the highest priority to the use of the Holy Bible in Burmese. But when it comes to the significance of the *Tripitaka*, the evaluation of Burmese people differed from that of the churches; whereas the churches considered the *Tripitaka* as one of the least useful media, the Burmese themselves pointed to it as one of the most significant, especially during the awareness phase.

The Burmese converts perceived that God spoke to them not only through church and its media and methods, but also through Buddhist scriptures, although the church had no intention of employing this media. This fact points out that the Burmese perceived God could communicate with them in any means with impact.

The role of the local congregations was considered to be very significant to all three phases by the Burmese Buddhist converts. In the awareness phase, the Holy Bible and certain passages of the *Tripitaka* were the most important media. Of the specifically Christian activities, intercessions and personal witness were appreciated most. Among the personal experiences, observing the life-style of Christians was the most important, and Christian ministers were the most influential persons.

In the conversion phases, the Holy Bible was the most important medium. Of the specifically Christian activities, intercession, prayer with Christians, and personal witness were considered to have had the strongest impact. Personal experiences, answered prayer, and observing the life-style of Christians were the most important. Also in this phase, non-Burmese Christian ministers were the most influential persons.

In the incorporation phase, the Holy Bible was the most important media. In this phase, the social services were estimated to have had more influence on the converts' spiritual journey. Of all the specifically Christian activities, intercessions and prayer with Christians were the most important. Of personal experiences, answered prayer and observing the life-style of Christians again had exerted the most influence on their spiritual journey. Non-Burmese Christian ministers were still the most important persons, but in this phase friends began to play a significant role.

The Context

The analysis of the survey indicated how the context of Burmese people and the context of the non-Burmese Christian community impacted the spiritual journey of the converts in various ways. Most obvious is the pressure from the converts' Buddhist families in particular and communities as well. Therefore it is not surprising that when the pressure was at its highest, in the conversion phase, a majority of the respondents felt that it had some or even much negative influence on their spiritual journey.

The negative impact of the Burmese Buddhist context is also seen in the problems that converts had concerning the Christian teaching about the crucifixion and Trinity, particularly in the awareness phase. In the Buddhist context, crucifixion is due to the fierce penalty of bad *kamma* and the concept of a Triune God is controversial. However, the negative influence of these teachings was significantly reduced over time in their spiritual journey.

The Result from the Understanding of the Gospel

From the data, it may be concluded that many Burmese understood the gospel, which was communicated to them, as in some ways related to their Buddhist religion. The aspects of the gospel (as they understood it) that attracted them most to Christianity, however, were exactly the teachings that differed most from Buddhist teaching.

Looking carefully at the result of the interaction of the Burmese with the gospel, the conversion of Burmese people to Christ is very small. As many as 58% of the respondents were baptized within the last seven years, but only 48% were baptized eight or more years ago. Although it was impossible to obtain precise and comprehensive data, it is fairly safe to conclude that the total number of adults baptized does not exceed 400 in all of the Yangon area. Accordingly, based on the data analysis, it may be concluded that the task of the communication of the gospel to the Burmese people in Yangon is not a people movement but a movement of individuals, as most have become Christians through contact with Christians from other ethnic groups. Over half of the respondents were young, with one-third under thirty when they became interested in the gospel and even at the time of their baptisms. And about one-tenth were under twenty when they expressed interest in Christ and were baptized.

The converts exhibited strong Christian beliefs and their cognitive, affective, and behavioral responses to the questions about Jesus Christ and forgiveness of sin were in harmony with traditional Christian theology and practice as found in Protestant churches in Yangon city. Only when it came to their relationship to Scripture, a significant minority had a more positive attitude toward the Buddhist scriptures (which diminished as the converts grew older in their faith) clearly related to the evangelistic use of some certain passages of *Tripitaka*.

The Burmese Buddhist converts had a strong identity as Christians, and the majority of them also had a strong relationship to the Christian community, but a significant minority faced serious problems of not feeling at home in the non-Burmese congregations. So it would be thought helpful for the Burmese Christians to have their own Burmese congregations. In their opinion, this would help them to feel more at home in the church, just as it would make it easier for other Burmese Buddhists to become followers of Christ.

All respondents were converted individually, and their conversion to Christianity mostly led to their separation from their family. Moreover, they still had a strong identity as "Burmese" and as Christian, but the majority of them had serious problems being accepted by their Burmese community. Based on these findings, it can be concluded that the primary method of evangelism used among the Burmese people has generally been 'extraction evangelism.'

Summary

In the analysis of the missions of Protestant churches in Yangon from twenty Christian leaders, it was concluded that their missions to a great extent were following traditional, non-contextualized mission principles and approaches. The analysis of the conversion to Christianity among the Burmese showed that none of the converts were members of contextual congregations and that all of them had been extracted from their community. These findings from field research reflect the fact that the churches in Yangon urgently need to develop a paradigm of Christian communication to communicate the gospel contextually in the Burmese Buddhist context. The following chapter will venture to develop it in the context of Yangon city.

CHAPTER 6

A Paradigm of Contextual Communication

Understanding the socio-cultural religious values of Burmese people and their worldview is vital in developing a paradigm of communication. While the lens of a paradigm may present the jewel of enlightenment, it limits the scope of research simultaneously. Ironically, the limiting of scope mentioned by Kuhn can be illustrated as an example of a group of people imprisoned in a larger box. The paradigm of the box will make it impossible to see outside of it. As there is no conceptual scheme or way to understand the world outside of the box (even though it may have an open lid), the understanding and scope of perception is limited from those within it (1970, 62-65).

Within the Burmese socio-cultural context in an urban setting, particularly in Yangon, I will develop a contextual communication paradigm. However, its scope will be shown to cover only three dimensions of missions within the Burmese Buddhist community in Yangon: Communication Strategies, Christological Message, and Ecclesiological Structure. These dimensions are related to each other, and reflect integration between awareness, conversion and incorporation of the converts into congregations in the local context.

Communicational Strategies

Originally, the word "strategy" was used as a military term. However, it also has a solid biblical precedent and it is of central importance for Christian communication (Sogaard 1993, 54). A communication strategy for each target people group must, increasingly, be shaped by the values, needs and style of its context. In this section, the proposed strategies for the effectiveness of Christian communication in the urban context of Burmese Buddhists are to be addressed as the primary task of the communicator, which is to communicate the gospel in a way that allows the Burmese Buddhists to engage Christ relationally.

As we discussed, contextual communication takes place when the communicators engage the receptors. Once they have engaged Christ relationally the cognitive implications of the gospel will be interpreted based on the quality of relationships. These relational issues shape the informational truth issues of the gospel for each context. In the reality of the communication process, the gospel does not call for objectivity in interpretation but calls us to interpret our context in terms of our relationship with Jesus Christ. Thus the task of communicator is to bring the receptors into relationship with the Creator through a relationship with Jesus Christ. This is a social message and can only be communicated in the midst of social relations. In Burmese society communicators must incarnate Jesus Christ following the socio-cultural and religious context. So in developing communication strategies for the Burmese Buddhists in Yangon the following key issues will be addressed as follows.

Family Networks for Communication through Family Networks

In Asian societies in general, the social solidarity is family-oriented with primarily religious communities (Yeo 1993, 126). This solidarity demands evangelization of whole families rather than individuals so that whole families and groups of families be won for Christ if viable churches are to be planted and are to make an adequate impact on the community. As pointed out earlier, the dominant issue in Burmese society is the interdependence of the social group. Seen from the social context, the influence of the group is strongest at the level of the household. Consequently, the first communicational strategy is within the social structure of the interdependent social group, giving special attention to the household. So communication of the gospel within the household in a Burmese context should be done within relationships.

As discussed in chapter 1, the goal of communication is conversion. To reach this goal, however, biblical evidence never seems to sanction confrontational means. Rather, it is *"processual"* (K Ng 1993, 188-189) through establishing rapport between communicator and recipient. This procession needs to happen even among the single family members throughout the course of gospel communication. Accordingly, the churches in Yangon must mark their relationship with others by living on behalf of others. In this way, communication must consist of not merely verbal enunciation of the truth, but the non-verbal message of the gospel or the demonstration of the truth as well. In this process, the non-verbal message of the gospel will be found more acceptable because it will affirm the group in morally powerful ways. Nida puts it this way:

> All divine communication is essentially incarnation for it comes not only in words, but also in life. Even if a truth is given only in words, it has no real validity until it has been translated into life. Only then does the Word of life become life to the receptor. The words are in a sense nothing in and of themselves. Even as wisdom is emptiness unless lived out in behavior, so the Word is void unless related to experience. In the incarnation of God in Jesus Christ, the Word (expression and revelation of the wisdom of God) became flesh. This same fundamental principle has been followed throughout the history of the church, for God has constantly chosen to use not only words but human beings as well to witness to his grace; not only the message but the messengers; not only the Bible but the church (1960, 226).

Nida's statement reinforces that relational communication comes not just from the lips, but also through the relational lifestyles of the communicators.

It reveals further that the church itself needs to be a message to the Burmese people in communication context.

This relational communication of the gospel within the social structure of Burmese society demands that the whole household unit be taken into account. Failure to bear this in mind very often has led households to ostracize, persecute, or even abandon individual converts from the family. In the Burmese context while the household unit, thus, should be the main focus, special attention should be given to the heads of the household. This does not mean that until the head of the household is converted, the churches keep sharing with him. But strategically within social structure, communication will be appropriate if the father or an elder in the Burmese family believes in and follows Christ as his disciple, followed by consultation with other members of the family so that they corporately decide to follow Jesus Christ, resulting in a Christian household. This will also be a means to avoid persecution as the head has authority in the family.

Patron-Client Communication

Communication within the household group also requires communication that follows the structure of Burmese relationships in terms of social values. This strategy requires structuring communication to flow in terms of older to younger relationships. So patron-client communication would be appropriate in the context of social values of Burmese people. Stephen Bailey states:

> Christian communicators will need to be concerned not only for the communication of information but also for the social obligations involved in the communication relationship. For the most part, Christian witness should flow from the older one in the relationship to the younger one. But older communicators will need to be aware of and live up to the social responsibility to provide advice and security for those who are younger. They should not be surprised when the younger one converts rather quickly. But neither should they be surprised if these younger converts abandon the faith just as quickly when

the older one ignores to provide the kind of care expected of them (2003, 164).

Due to the high regard for social values in Southeast Asia's Buddhist societies, Bailey's statement is also applicable to Burmese Buddhist contexts in developing communication strategies. Christian communicators (foreign missionaries and local Christians in Myanmar) should consider social obligations carefully as they can create problems by establishing expectations they cannot live up to in the long-term. On the other hand, to effect contextual conversion, in reality the churches must instruct the new converts to give their allegiance to the household to which they belong. Of course, living up to their obligations in their household is important for four reasons: 1) the Scriptures teach us to honor our fathers and mothers so that things will go well with us (Eph 6:2); 2) it is also one of the social duties of children in a Burmese social context; 3) it can be a means of avoiding persecution for the wrong reasons, and 4) it can also be a means of winning some special space necessary for further Christian witness.

Communication through Burmese Religious and Cultural Practices

Every month, the Myanmar lunar calendar has traditional festivals which people celebrate with other members of the society (Nyunt 2005, 9-11). Each festival that falls in each month has significance in the cultural-religious context. There is no space to elucidate the significance of each festival. The first and most important factor among them, however, is the social gathering and religion-fostering function of the feast, as people gather irrespective of their social differences. On the occasions, usually people do merits by donating money and gifts to Buddhist monks and for the decoration of religious buildings, and Buddhist monks tell stories from the Buddhist scripture. It is an appropriate time to attend the ritual as an observer to take advantage of such indirect Christian witness. Of course, communication is dynamically creative. Further, in the socio-cultural context, the Burmese style of relationship functions through a strong self-identity, grateful relationships, smooth interpersonal relationships, flexibility and adjustment, and interdependence as stated in previous chapters. To have deep relational bonding requires participation in the communal activities, sharing difficult experiences in the natural pattern of life, and togetherness and long-term commitment (Myaing 1991, 23-79).

The churches in Yangon, however, are consistently instructed not to participate in the traditional rituals of Buddhists. Many Christians obey the instruction of the Protestant churches and end up cutting themselves off, or seriously straining their relationships. Zau Lat calls them "self-contained kinds of churches" establishing "mission compound mentality" as stated earlier. The churches are eager to share the gospel with those who come to church as visitors, and thus limiting their mission work *in the world*.

On a social level this practice cuts off opportunities for further witness that would naturally be there through group relationships. Failure to participate in traditional Burmese rituals communicates that a person has opted out of the group. The implication is that a person no longer feels obligated to the needs of the group. But they unintentionally ignore that communication is for communion and in religion we witness a divine-human communication and the cultivation of relationships. Religious communication is thus both vertical (between God and human beings) and horizontal (between human beings). Van Baal and Van Beek state that, "religion is a system of symbols by which . . . (a human being) communicates with his universe" (1985, ix). All human communication thus takes place through the sharing of meanings in common symbols. In this context Carey's redefinition of communication in "ritualistic" terms is significant (1975, 1-23).

M. Gurevitch J. Curran and J. Woolacott state:

> A ritual view of communication is not directed toward the extension of message in space, but the maintenance of society in time; not the act of imparting information or influence, but the creation, presentation, and celebration of shared beliefs. If a transmission view of communication centers on the extension of message across geography for purposes of control, a ritual view centers on the sacred ceremony which draws persons together in fellowship and communality (1977, 412).

The ritual view focuses on the notion of cultural sharing and the maintenance of family and society. The key word here is 'culture,' understood as a symbolic container, or a 'system of meanings,' in which reality is constructed, maintained and transformed. Accordingly, anthropologists treat religion as a cultural phenomenon and as an expression of the human mind in various cultures. In this sense, the word "culture" directs us to the study of an entire way of life. These insights from cultural anthropology make clear that communication in the religious context focuses on the transmission of attitudes and values created or discovered. This intergenerational transmission is evidenced in the family and community context in Myanmar.

In contextual communication, the media that communicators employ plays an important role. In a Burmese socio-cultural context, strong kinship (household) level relationships are the most effective media for communication of the gospel to the Burmese Buddhist people. The gospel is a relational message that requires a covenant between humans and the Creator, and covenant keeping with each other. Spiritual power and cognitive truth will also be involved in communicating the gospel to the Burmese people. How the power and truth of the gospel are interpreted, however, depends upon how our Christian communicators engage others relationally. To engage relations with Burmese people contextually, in the following section we will see the content of the gospel message in the Burmese Buddhist context.

Christological Message

We seek to communicate the gospel effectively by remaining faithful to the intent of Scripture and relevant to the audience, using media and styles appropriate to particular contacts. As DT Nile asserts, we are called to make the gospel understandable to the audience (Niles 1968, 30). The primary purpose of this section is to close the gap successfully between communicators and the members of the audience through the Christological message. Now, it is more important to draw out the *sine qua non* essentials of our message. According to John T Seamands, the effective communication of the gospel varies depending on who is giving it to whom and where and how (2000, 11). When attempting to apply the gospel to the context of Burmese Buddhism, what do Burmese Buddhists want to hear from the communicator? It is liberation from a *samsaric* existence because their ultimate goal is to attain *nibbana*. In this regard, a well-known monk K Sri Dhammananda states:

> Each and every person must make the effort to train and purify himself toward attaining his or her own salvation by following the guidance given by the Buddha. You yourself make the effort for your salvation; the Buddhas are only Teachers who can show you how to achieve it (2002, 25-26).

Attaining the *nibbana,* Buddhists must rely entirely on themselves, not on any external god, savior, or even the Buddha. That is, one must overcome one's own accumulated *kamma* alone. In this regard, attaining *nibbana* or salvation for the Buddhists is the extinction of the fires of greed, hatred and delusion and consequently the deliverance from *samsara*, the cycle of rebirth. The only way to extinguish these desires is to know "the Four Noble Truths." Based on these Four Noble Truths Buddha laid out the essential framework upon which all his later teachings were based. He taught these truths not as metaphysical theories or as articles of faith, but as categories by which we should frame our direct experiences in a way that is conducive to Awakening. The process can be done through following the Eightfold Path categorized into Morality (*Sila*), Concentration (*Samadhi*) and Wisdom (*Panna*). On the other hand, Buddha has said that if anyone fails to understand these Four Truths, he or she will be continually in the cycle of birth and death. To clarify this concept, the venerable Webu Sayadaw states:

> Because of our ignorance (*avijja*) of these Noble Truths, because of our inexperience in framing the world in their terms, we remain bound to *samsara*, the wearisome cycle of birth, aging, illness, death, and rebirth. Craving propels this process onward, from one moment to the next and over the course of countless lifetimes, in accordance with *kamma*, the universal

law of cause and effect. According to this immutable law, every action that one performs in the present moment – whether by body, speech, or mind itself – eventually bears fruit according to its skillfulness and happiness will ultimately ensure. As long as one remains ignorant of this principle, one is doomed to an aimless existence: happy one moment, in despair the next; enjoying one lifetime in good place, the next in hell in the circle of *samsara* (1997, 6-7).

According to the Buddhist view of salvation, it is ascertained that Buddha's instruction to his followers is to save themselves through their own efforts. Accordingly, anyone who pursues liberation must follow this path 24 hours without termination every day. Whoever fails is doomed to an aimless existence in *samsara* (Ibid., 1997, 6). Critically speaking, it is only an evolutionary process to be achieved by non-theistic ethical disciplines, a system of self-training, anthropocentric, stressing ethics to the exclusion of theology. Probably, he might be silent as to any future life, putting a minimum of positive content into his conception of *nibbana* as he offered neither redemption nor forgiveness of sin. Optimistically, his instruction helps us to realize the greatness of sin, the difference between sin and virtue, and the way to get rid of sin. This point is in line with an interview between Buddha and Brahman about how to be liberated from *samsara* or salvation. The following is a quotation from the Buddhist scripture:

> Even though you give alms, observe the five commandments governing everyone, the eight commandments governing a fervent Buddhist and the 227 commandments governing the conduct of a buddhist, join your hands in prayer a billion times, and meditate five times a day, you will not be saved. Even if you do these things every day, you will only receive merit equal to one eighth of a split hair. Even the baby which is still in its mother's womb cannot go to the gate of heaven . . . Man's sins are so many, so heavy, heavier than the sky, thicker than the earth, higher than the great stone, filling all four corners to the thickness of a cubit. If the angel comes

once a year and lightly wipes the stone one time, when the stone has been completely wiped away and disappears, then will the sin be gone (Inta Chanthavongsouk 1999, 25).

This discussion emphasizes that Buddha himself realizes bad *kamma* are equated with sin and it is far too great to be compared with anything through the illustration "sin is heavier than the sky, thicker than earth." This is true because true sins are humankind's wrong actions against God when they do not obey and do not honor him as Creator (Rom 1:21). They sinned by obeying Satan in Genesis 3:1-7 and worshiped the things of God's creation instead of worshiping him (Rom 1:21-25). This is the great sin that humankind did which brought punishment of death and no human is able to wash away that sin. That is why all people in all nations of the world need salvation from sin. The Buddha explained clearly the difference between sin and virtue and that virtue cannot subtract from the sin no matter how much we do. So, whoever depends on one's own virtue to save one's self from sin is depending on the wrong thing and is contrary to Buddha's teaching. It is impossible to wash sin away by good works and deeds of merit or non-theistic ethical disciplines. Almost certainly, the reason Buddha spoke to Ananda, one of his first five disciples, about a future Buddha known as *Arit Metteyya* was because he said:

> I am not the first Buddha to come on earth, nor shall I be the last. In due time, another Buddha will arise in this world, a Holy One, a Supremely Enlightened One, endowed with wisdom, in conduct auspicious, knowing the universe, an incomparable leader of men, a master of devas and men. He will reveal to you the same Eternal Truths, which I have taught you. He will proclaim a religious life, wholly perfect and pure; such as I now proclaim (Dhammananda 2002, 60).

Of this future Savior, Inta Chanthavongsouk writes:

You must give alms and search for another God that will come to save the world and will help you afterward. His name is *Arit Mettayya*. He was before me but will come after me. In the Savior who will come to save the world, you will see puncture wounds like a wheel in the palms of his hands, and the bottom of his feet. In his side there is the mark of a stab wound, and his forehead is full of scars. This God will be the big ark that will lead you to cross the cycle of birth and death to Nirvana. Do not prefer the old way. You will not be saved. You must get rid of the old way and you will have a new spirit which looks like the firefly and comes from above to live in your heart and continues to live in this world and in eternity (1999, 25-26).

According to the redemptive analogy of the teachings of Buddhist scripture and the investigation of two authors Dhammananda and Inta, it is clear that Buddha said that "sinners cannot help themselves to get rid of sin" as salvation is not from him but from the one who will come after him; the Messiah or Savior who has great mercy on sinners (see Rom 5:8). Those who take refuge in him will not perish but will live in this world and in eternity (John 3:16, 5:24; 1 John 4:7). That is, "the big ark" refers to the compassionate Savior Jesus who is the way leading us to the city of *nibbana*. In addition, it refers to the access-platform of the greatness of God's way, which has no limitation but is big enough for all, including Burmese Buddhists, to enter. Those who enter the ark will have access to go to the city of *nibbana* (Rev 21:1-4) where the compassionate Savior comes. I will also illustrate through the following diagram what Burmese Buddhists need to clearly hear in order to know that Jesus Christ is the Liberator, the compassionate Savior who is coming outside of *samsara*.

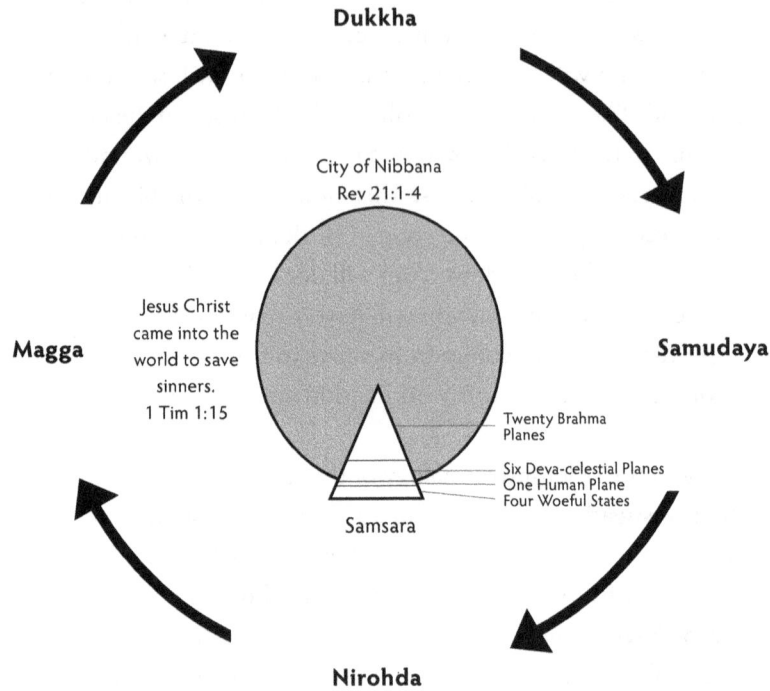

DIAGRAM 1: Jesus as Liberator from Samsara

This diagram shows that Buddhists are pursuing liberation through self-effort. But distraction at the time of concentration at the *Magga* stage shows a sinful human cannot concentrate without termination. He or she remains bound to *samsara* (thirty-one planes of existence: four woeful states, one human plane, six planes of *deva* and twenty planes of Brahma—see the diagram). It clearly shows that salvation is impossible through human efforts but only through the One who comes from outside of *samsara*. And those who take refuge in him have the chance to obtain the "*nibbana*," or the liberation of *samsara*. Based on the facts stated earlier, I will conclude my christological message for the Burmese Buddhists. This will open new ways of introducing Jesus Christ to Burmese Buddhists, and open new ways in which Buddhists can express their faith in Christ.

Firstly, all peoples in all nations of the world need the salvation of Christ. Religion, or belief, desires salvation from sin, because it is the ultimate goal of humankind in their religious beliefs. For the Buddhists, salvation or liberation is based on the Law of *Kamma*, cause and effect as stated earlier. It is an ethical retribution through Morality (*Sila*), Concentration (*Samadhi*) and Wisdom (*Panna*). There is no principle of grace or forgiveness, strictly speaking. It is a single reality, which is in process (*samsara*). In other words, it is a central concept related to the Buddhist scheme of liberation. The belief is that merits or demerits are accumulated in one's life according to the good or evil deeds that one does. No deity oversees this operation. It rather is the net effect of this phenomenon that determines one's *kammic* destiny and afterlife. In the practice of their religious values, however, Burmese Buddhists believe that merit accumulation is not something that can only be done for oneself, but can be extended to others, too, and even to the departed dead through charitable acts. This transference of merit from the living to the dead catalyzes the attainment of liberation (*nibbana*). We can use this merit transference concept as a bridge to the experience of the cross. "Savior who will come . . . , you will see puncture wounds like a wheel in the palms of his hands, . . . full of scars." In this prophecy of Buddha, the Lord Jesus Christ is presented as the one who accumulated infinite merits by virtue of his sinless life and meritorious death. Since he was perfect in his nature, he generated an infinite number of merits during his earthly life and ministry through his innumerable good deeds (John 21:25). Even though the death of Jesus on the cross generated an infinite amount of merit, what effect could it have on humanity? According to the Buddhist merit-transference (*pattidana*) concept, living beings have the ability to transfer merit to deceased persons on the basis of charitable deeds. If human beings who are laden with evil and are also unenlightened are believed to be capable of transferring merit, it is not incomprehensible at all that the Lord Jesus Christ would be able to transfer his merit to others. In fact the argument holds that when it comes to the transference of merit, it may only be possible for a perfect being who has no sin within himself to really do so and comes from outside of *samsaric* existence.

This is in line with communicative styles in Asian cultures, which will bring up the most important insights at a later stage in the discourse.

Therefore, the message of the compassionate Savior Jesus Christ may be introduced in a cyclical fashion. Starting with his incarnation coming from outside of *samsara* (1 Tim 1: 15) to overcoming the law of *kamma* by his holy life, death, resurrection, ascension; readiness to help us, and his promise to return to earth in order to receive those who put their trust in him.

Ecclesiastical Structure

I propose contextual communication strategies and content of the message which are relevant in the Burmese Buddhist context. As communication is a process, once there is receptivity to our evangelistic message, the next step is to nurture our converts in such a way that they develop a new communion in their own cultural context.

Ever since the inception of the church, the nature of the church—its essence, attributes, marks, criteria, symbols, signs, and distinguishing features—has been debated. Looking at the church's nature from the standpoint of a "becoming-essence," Charles E Van Engen sees the church as an emerging observable reality, which is in the process of becoming in reality what it is in faith (1981, 62). What then constitutes the church? Since the church is at the same time visible and hidden, and since the church is always in the process of becoming what it already is, we must look for "open concepts"—windows, signs or pointers to the reality of the church that may not be definitively described or defined. However, in order to be able to use the concept of the church in the analyses of this study, it is necessary as far as possible to identify some concrete, visible and tangible characteristics (Ibid., 406-407).

In one of the key passages where Jesus talks about the future church, he concludes by stating that "where two or three come together in my name, there am I with them" (Matt 18:15-20), or in the stronger words of the King James Version, "where two or three are gathered in my name, there am I in the midst of them." The thing that qualifies a gathering of people to be the church is the presence of Jesus Christ in their midst.

The church was born on the day of Pentecost. The significance of Pentecost is that Christ came to be present among his disciples through his Holy Spirit. After that, whenever the disciples gathered in the name of Jesus Christ, he was present in their midst through his Spirit, continuing the work he had done among them in the flesh, now through his body the church. The church therefore happens when and where Christ, according to the Bible, has promised his presence to his disciples. Following this understanding, the true church may therefore be identified by the following signs: a gathering of people in the name of Jesus Christ, the preaching point of the Word of Jesus Christ, the sacrament of baptism and Holy Communion, the demonstration of love among the members, an agent to continue God's missions. All six of the signs of the true church are demonstrated in the life and ministry of the apostolic church described in Acts 2: the fellowship (v 42), the word (v 42), the sacraments (vv 41-42), the unity in love (v 44), prayers (v 42), and mission (v 45 and v 47). These six characteristics, which point to the presence of Jesus Christ in a gathering of people, will be used in evaluating existing local congregations in a contextual nature. And new models for local congregations as contextual congregations will be evaluated on the basis of whether they further or hinder the development of these characteristics.

Alternative Models of Contextual Local Congregations

When developing alternative contextual models of congregations, the focus will not be primarily on cultural forms but on sociological aspects of the context—on community, organization, and identity. Seen from this perspective, the local congregation is the sociological platform on the basis of which the Burmese people will live their social life as Christians, and on the basis of which they can develop their contextual worship and fellowships, and their contextual theology. At the same time, the local congregation will function as a plausible structure for the maintenance and development of the religious and ethnic identity of the Burmese converts. Combining all these sociological perspectives into a set of five questions, it is appropriate to differentiate between types of local congregations for Burmese contexts.

1. With whom do the Burmese converts gather? The Burmese converts either gather with members of a congregation dominated by non-Burmese Christians and thereby become a member of the non-Burmese Christian community, or

they gather only with other Burmese Christians and thereby communicate that they still belong to the Burmese community.
2. Where do the Burmese converts gather? In the Yangon context, churches and monasteries are high profile religious buildings closely identified with specific religious communities. Therefore it is of critical importance whether Burmese converts gather in a church building, or in a private home (a house fellowship).
3. What religious identity do the Burmese converts subscribe to? In a Buddhist context the term "Christian" may often connote treason to the Buddhist community and attachment to Western religious values. The Burmese converts may therefore choose between the traditional term, "Christian," which identifies them with non-Burmese Christians, or they may select a term that indicates that they are termed as examples of "followers of the compassionate Savior" or "followers of *Arit Metteyya*."
4. Do the Burmese converts have a single religious organizational membership or a double membership? What is at stake here is whether the Burmese converts, who gather with other believers in Jesus, will at the same time continue to participate in any of the Buddhist religious activities.
5. How openly do the Burmese converts gather? The question here is whether they will gather in congregations publicly, or whether they will form underground congregations that meet secretly.

Using the above questions in defining models of congregations for Burmese people, it is possible to differentiate between the following six types of congregations:

1. A Traditional non-Burmese church. This is a congregation whose members belong to one or more non-Burmese ethnic groups, all of whom come from a non-Buddhist religious background. The members worship publicly in a traditional church building.
2. A Burmese church. This is a local congregation whose members are Burmese people. They worship publicly in their own church building. The congregation is typically much bigger than that of house fellowships. Their religious identity is Christian, and

they do not participate in Buddhist worship particularly in the monastery.

3. A Burmese House Fellowship. This is a local congregation whose members are Burmese people. They worship publicly, but with a much lower profile than the Burmese church, as they are a house fellowship that meets in the home of one of the members. The house fellowship can be as small as two to three members, but not larger than can be accommodated in a Burmese home without attracting too much attention from the Burmese Buddhist community. The religious identity of the members is Christian, and they do not participate in Burmese worship in the monastery.

4. A Community of followers of *Arit Metteyya* Buddha. This is a local congregation whose members are Burmese people. They worship publicly in an appropriate place and follow a Buddhist monastery style of worship. Their identity is Buddhist devotees to *Arit Metteyya* Buddha, but they do not participate in the Buddhist worship in the traditional monastery.

5. A House Fellowship of *Arit Metteyya* Buddhists. This is a local congregation whose members are Burmese people. They worship publicly, but with a much lower profile than those of the *Arit Metteyya* Buddhist model, as they are a house fellowship. The house fellowship can be as small as two to three members, but not larger than can be accommodated in a Burmese home without attracting too much attention from the Burmese Buddhist community. Their identity is devotees of *Arit Metteyya* Buddha, and they participate in the Buddhist worship in the monastery.

6. An underground Burmese House Fellowship. This is a local congregation whose members are Burmese people. They worship secretly as a house fellowship in the home of one of the members. The underground house fellowship can be as small as two to three members, but not larger than can be accommodated in a Burmese home without endangering their secret status. Their secret identity is Christian or *Arit Metteyya* Buddhist, but their

public identity is Buddhists. They also participate in the religious activities of Buddhist society.

An Ecclesiological Evaluation of the Congregational Models

Out of the six congregational models, the traditional non-Burmese church model is popular in Yangon particularly with mainline churches. Apart from this model, the ecclesiological validity of all these types of congregations has been hotly debated. As stated, the ecclesiological structure of the church in Myanmar is still western-oriented within the different denominations. In the following, I will look at the Homogenous Unit Principle (HUP), which applies to all the alternative five models. Then the two *Arit Metteyya* Buddhist models (4 & 5) and the underground congregation model (6) will be considered separately. Finally, I will assess the validity of the forms of house fellowship: underground, *Arit Metteyya* Buddhist and traditional.

All models of local congregations, apart from the traditional non-Burmese church model, follow the HUP. Here, however, I will discuss the HUP in relation to the Burmese church and the Burmese house fellowship models. HUP has been used in church planting among the minority ethnic groups (i.e., Chin, Kachin, Kayin) all over the country of Myanmar but not among the Burmese people so far.

Ever since the father of the church growth movement, McGavran, in 1955 wrote his famous book, *The Bridges of God*, in which he claimed that "people become Christian fastest, when least change of race or clan is involved" (1995, 23), the ecclesiological validity of the HUP for mission and church planting has been discussed among theologians and missiologists. Questions such as "Is a HUP local congregation a true church?" have been asked. The sign of the true church that is at stake here is the unity of the church. The "unity of love," which characterizes the true church, may be present in such congregations provided that two conditions are respected. Referring to a church for converts from Buddhism, the first condition, stating that in a "homogenous church, there would not be a bar to others from disparate backgrounds joining the church. The doors would be open to all. But the flavor of the church would be distinctive and would thus naturally attract mostly converts from Buddhism" (Parshall 1984, 160-161). The other condition is that such a Burmese church or house fellowship should endeavor to live in fellowship, not only with other Burmese congregations, but also with non-Burmese congregations recognized as the body of Christ. Commenting on the apostle Paul's mission principles, Gilliland concludes: The unity of the church – the fact that in Christ all people are brought together – is not denigrated or contradicted by the homogenous way in which people most frequently become Christian . . . Paul could see that it was natural for people to come to Christ together with their own kind. It is not to say this is the ideal, for the gospel unites all races and all peoples into one body. But to utilize the differences for discipling, that is, bringing people to Christ in response to the Great Commission is in harmony with Paul's approach. Furthermore, though the application of the HUP may be necessary and biblically valid step in evangelizing a people, it is also true that by beginning with a homogeneous group, we do not arrive at a picture of what the church is meant to be in the final sense. It must, in maturing, move toward a heterogeneous scriptural ideal, which is truly oneness in Christ, and which includes all differences, even while superseding them (1998, 206). The *Arit Metteyya* Buddhist congregations may take at least two forms, either as an *Arit Mettayya* Buddhist community or as an *Arit Mettayya* house fellowship. The ecclesiological issue at stake in this type of congregation is whether the members can be said to be truly gathering in the name of Jesus Christ and holding fast to the word of Jesus Christ when they have not made a clean break with Buddhism and the Buddhist community. Are such congregations valid as Christian congregations or are their members trapped in syncretism?

As churches in Myanmar are very conservative in practical lifestyle and living in a majority Buddhist society, it is certain that Christian leaders will totally reject this approach because they consider the venture to be syncretistic. But it is valid to distinguish between religious and cultural forms and structures, and commitments and faith allegiances, so the Buddhist worship forms may be utilized in a genuine worship of God in Jesus Christ.

Three of the five proposed models of local congregations are house fellowships. What distinguishes house fellowships from more traditional congregations are normally their meeting place and their size. Instead of gathering in publicly dedicated church buildings, they meet in private homes. While most denominations in Yangon require a certain number of adult members, often fifteen or more, in order to be accepted as a local congregation, house fellowships are often much smaller. Altogether, house fellowships have a lower degree of institutionalization than more traditional churches.

According to my understanding of the nature of the true church, however, the church is neither identified with a building or certain activities in a building; the church, rather, is a people of God. What constitutes the people of God is, thus, not a certain number. House churches or house fellowships are not a new invention; they represent the typical model of a local congregation into which converts were incorporated following the missionary work of Paul.

> The most important feature of the church was the multitude of small units, each of which met together, working out its new life in sharing blessings and working through problems. It is error to think even of Paul's urban churches as large single congregations. They were, on the contrary, gatherings of God's people who shared similar lives, people who related naturally to each other, and who corporately were, in fact, expressions of the diversity of the people of God (Ibid., 209).

Roland Allen recommended that mission organizations consider the same model. Without using the term house fellowships, he advocated "the requirement of small native congregations of Christians with full power and authority as local churches" (1984, 3). Allen was concerned that due to ecclesiological and missionary traditions, new believers in the mission were not soon enough gathered in authentic "native" congregations and were deprived of the sacraments. With his strong emphasis on ordained ministry, Allen suggested that a small group of new believers be immediately formed into a local congregation in which one of the new believers was given basic instruction to enable him to administer the sacraments without any dependence on a pastor from another congregation. Such a person would then be ordained by a bishop to be an unpaid minister for his own people (Ibid., 117-136).

Based on the example of Paul's mission and my understanding of what the church is, I agree with Allen that even a small group of believers may form a local congregation with all the necessary functions, including the administration of the sacraments. The conclusion, therefore, is that local congregations following any one of the five alternative models of contextualized congregations, may be ecclesiologically valid. The question is, however, which of these models are contextually relevant in Yangon today.

Contextual Evaluation of the Congregational Models

The contextual feasibility of these five models of local congregations must be determined. This will be done by an evaluation of each model on the basis of the critical aspects of the context in which they are to function. When analyzing whether these five models of local congregations fit into the context, four aspects of the context have to be taken into consideration.

1. The Yangon Context. Most congregations in Yangon are geared to the needs of poor people. When choosing a congregational model to be used in Burmese missions, the Burmese lifestyle must be considered.
2. The Burmese Buddhist Context. They are converts from Buddhism, and although they have become Christians, they are still influenced by their Buddhist background. Furthermore, the Christian-Buddhist relations in Yangon today have to be considered when discussing the type of congregation that will be most relevant.
3. The Church Context. In the final analysis, the choice of a model of local congregation for the Burmese converts belongs to the churches in Yangon. Therefore the theology, the tradition, and other attitudes of these churches have to be considered so that the model which is recommended may be acceptable to the decision-makers in the churches.
4. The Burmese converts' context. Finally, the characteristics of the Burmese converts, which have been analyzed in this research, are

very significant, because these converts will be the kernels of the new Burmese congregations.

All five models envisage separate local congregations for Burmese people in accordance with field survey research. This is in harmony with the wishes of the Burmese converts, the majority of whom stated that they thought that it would be helpful for Burmese Christians to have their own Burmese congregations. Worshiping in the Burmese language and having fellowship in ways that are appropriate for Burmese people would also make it easier for other Burmese people to join such congregations.

The study of the history of Burmese mission and the interviews with church leaders in Yangon showed that there are no Burmese congregations established in Yangon city. Although there may be a few hundred converts in the Yangon municipal area, there are too few Burmese converts in one place to start Burmese churches like the other minority peoples. This may be a reason for the lack of Burmese congregations in Yangon.

The Buddhistic identity of a person in the Burmese context in Yangon is attached to his or her participation in the Buddhist monastic worship activities. The field research also showed that those Burmese people who publicly declared their faith in Christ and were baptized rejected the idea of continuing to perform Buddhist activities. To practice these activities would be tantamount to compromising their faith. Moreover, it can create conflict between Buddhists and Burmese Buddhist converts. Therefore the conclusion is that *Arit Metteyya* Buddhist congregation models are not feasible in the present Burmese context in Yangon.

The presence of significant numbers of secret believers among the Burmese people may speak for the establishment of underground congregations. If secret believers join a house fellowship in secret, they may not endanger their full membership of the Burmese community, and they may not lose their family. They have to continue to participate in the traditional ritual activities occasionally in order to be accepted in the community, while they meet with other Jesus believers in secret. Being full members of their Burmese community, they are in a much better position to witness effectively about Jesus to their Burmese relatives, neighbors and friends than are the Burmese converts in the traditional non-Burmese churches. They can witness through their lifestyle as stated in previous section. Exercising great care and selectivity, they may sometimes also witness in words to individuals in private sections.

If the cover of the secret believer or the underground congregation is "blown," these no-longer-secret believers can join an overt Burmese congregation or turn their own fellowship into an open congregation. After some time, secret believers may want to come out in the open with their new faith in Jesus. In both cases, underground house fellowships may give Burmese Buddhist seekers and converts time to get to know Christ and the body of Christ without being immediately expelled from their community. Ideally, by the time secret believers go public, if they ever choose to do so, they may have grown in their faith so much that they are in better position to cope with the pressure and persecution that may follow. Furthermore, they will have lived as believers in Jesus for a period (from months to years) together with their own people, who will have observed the change in their life due to their conversion. Though the secret believers' change of allegiance to Jesus Christ on a worldview level and their fellowship with other believers was invisible, the ensuring changes in their behavior, attitude and understanding hopefully will have been perceived and hopefully appreciated by the community, so that when they openly confess their belief in *Arit Metteyya* as their Savior, the rupture with and alienation from their community will be less drastic and painful for all those involved.

Whereas underground congregations may meet the needs of the secret believers in the Burmese context, most of the church-focused missions to Burmese people would probably not accept secret congregations as part of their mission strategy. First, there is no tradition in Yangon for secret congregations; congregations are considered to be public fellowships. Second, they may be suspected unnecessarily due to political instability.

There seems, however, to be an acceptance in the churches of the possibility of a person being a secret believer, and a willingness to work with secret believers. Whereas an official strategy of working towards the establishment of underground congregations is not feasible, it may be possible to gain acceptance for the idea of a temporary status of secrecy for individuals and small groups of Burmese people.

When the Burmese Buddhist context is considered, a Burmese house fellowship has a significant advantage. The small size of the fellowship and its informal structure contributes to the low profile of such a congregation. This can be compared to Massey's persuasive argument for church planting in a Muslim context. In such a profile of a congregation, Burmese converts and Buddhist seekers can meet for worship and will probably make such a congregation less offensive to the Burmese community. Attending such a house fellowship once a week can hardly lead to persecution and exclusion from the community. On the other hand, if persecution breaks out or if members find themselves in a serious emergency, such a fellowship may not be enough to support, assist and protect its members. Therefore, a Burmese house fellowship may need to join together in a network of Burmese fellowships that will take responsibility for each other's needs. Furthermore, although a Burmese house fellowship is an independent local congregation, it needs to be in fellowship with the surrounding non-Burmese churches and depend on their help and assistance.

A Burmese house fellowship seems to be very relevant to the situation of the present Burmese converts. The survey showed that the majority of the converts were from different parts of the Yangon municipal area. This means that there are too few Burmese converts in each location to form a Burmese congregation built on a traditional model. A house fellowship, however, can consist of as few as a two or three Burmese converts gathering in the name of Jesus Christ, who has promised his presence among them. In many cases, however, there might be a need for assistance from a Burmese or non-Burmese mature Christian in developing this fellowship. Until one of the Burmese members of the fellowship is discipled and trained up to take the role of spiritual leadership, the group will be led by this mature Christian. The house fellowship can meet at times and places that are convenient for the members and worship in ways that are meaningful to the Burmese people.

The need for Burmese converts in the small house fellowship to experience Christian fellowship and celebration in larger settings may be met by participation in occasional gatherings led by leaders and by bringing neighboring Burmese house fellowships together for joint meetings. This fellowship must also have access to baptism and Holy Communion; these rites could either be conducted by the leader or by a visiting pastor, according to the tradition of the denomination.

If the leadership of the churches understands the rationale behind the Burmese house fellowships, they should be able to accept Burmese house fellowships and incorporate them in their mission strategy without changing any of their basic ecclesiastical principles. The Burmese house fellowship is a flexible model of a local congregation. If the pressure from the Burmese Buddhists community grows very intense, new members of the house fellowship may remain secret believers for some time, or the whole house fellowship may go underground until the persecution subsides. On the other hand, if the house fellowship grows or experiences a local people movement, it may transform itself into a more institutionalized congregation with a church building (a Burmese church).

Summary

For the effective Christian communication of the gospel to Burmese Buddhists in an urban setting, in this chapter I ventured to propose the communicational strategies and content of the message needed to be relevant in the frame of reference. As mentioned in chapter 1, in the theoretical framework for this study, the goal of the communication is not only conversion, but also the incorporation of the converts into local congregations or the establishment of new congregations. For the purpose of establishing new congregations in the Burmese context, the five alternative models of contextual congregations were developed. The five models are still strange for the churches in Yangon by and large. But the ecclesiological principles involved in these congregational models were evaluated on the basis of the signs of a true church.

The evaluation of the feasibility of these five congregational models in relation to a Yangon Burmese Buddhist context, and the context of the church and the Burmese converts, showed that a community or fellowship of *Arit Metteyya* Buddha models should not be recommended. The Burmese church model is only relevant in cases where many Burmese people are converted in the same place, and the underground congregation model should only be considered as a temporary model. The best congregational model was the very flexible Burmese house fellowship model. The implementation of this congregational model may not solve all problems concerning the extraction of Burmese converts from their community and culture, but it seems likely that it will reduce and postpone some of the problems. At the same time, this model will provide the Burmese converts with a sociological platform on which they can address all the other contextual issues relating to their life in a Christian congregation.

CHAPTER 7

Recommendations and Conclusions

In this concluding chapter, I will draw out the missiological implications of my study for mission among the Burmese people. I do not recommend one specific issue but will identify the crucial issues that will have to be addressed when churches and mission organizations consider contextual communication of the gospel to Burmese people in Yangon. In chapter 1, several factors were identified as influencing the communication process: the communicator, the message, the channel, the understanding of the message by the receptor, the receptor, the response of the receptor, and the context.

The issues, according to this study, which seem to be of critical importance for an effective communication of the gospel to the Burmese Buddhists, will be presented in the form of ten key recommendations or missiological implications. Each is like a pearl that has grown through irritation and pain. Strung together, these pearls may provide helpful keys for strategizing ministries among the Burmese Buddhists in particular.

Recommendations

While the communicator must clearly understand his biblical message, it is essential that he listen to the receptor for feedback that will clarify what is actually being understood. This cyclical feedback process will help clarify the conceptualization of the gospel and what the actual response time is. Reaching people at their level of understanding and listening to how God is working in their lives step-by-step always makes for good evangelism no matter how long it takes. That is why communicators should observe carefully and listen conscientiously to the heartbeat of the receptors. Research and surveys are needed to discover the deep-felt needs of the targeted people group. We must find out where people are itching and then scratch there with the gospel. Theologizing divorced from the real needs of people is futile. Thus, effective communication also needs indigenous forms, symbols, analogy, stories and word pictures of the target audience. The use of appropriate media such as ethnic song and music, indigenous dance-drama, and other arts as oral communication modes should be investigated and adapted for Christian witness and teaching.

More studies need to be made on points of contact related to the felt needs of the Burmese people. Ethical and moral similarities are used as the basis for presenting Christ. In fact, most of the felt needs of Burmese Buddhists in Yangon are in the bondage of *kammic* fatalism and the uncertainty of hope for the future. In this regard, the doctrine of *kamma* as dealing with an absolute falsehood, its incompleteness should be the contact point to find its fulfillment in Christ. Therefore, the application of the gospel concerning their felt needs gives possible clues for approaching the Burmese Buddhists in Yangon city.

This missiological implication is to encourage Burmese converts to remain connected to their household, community and other significant relationships. Many of the pioneer attempts of the Protestant Christians in Yangon included uprooting the Burmese converts from their natural surrounding and placing them in a foreign environment. It was intended to shelter them from persecution and ostracism by their own family and kinsmen and community, but it projects a picture of the gospel as foreign to the community as well as to the Burmese Buddhist converts. Consequently, the converts became estranged from members of their own household, kin group and community. Socially and culturally the new converts are disconnected from their network of trust relationships and perceived as traitors. They are also displaced from group (community) solidarity and social harmony. Thus, the new converts lose the chance of maintaining the vital relationships for reaching the family, kinsmen/women and community. In addition, they probably would not be welcomed back to the community unless they were willing to participate in its religious rituals, ceremonies and festivals, which are required of every good member of the community. The separation of the converts from their family and community has brought much pain to them and left the local churches with many difficult problems as well. At the same time the separation of the Burmese converts from their community and their Burmese lifestyle has impeded the spread of the gospel among the Burmese people.

In view of these facts, the Christian communicator should encourage the converts to remain connected to their network of relationships, members of their household, kin group and community. As difficult as it may be, the convert's presence in his household, kin group and community will build an essential bridge over which the gospel can flow. Also, it will remove the perception that Christianity is a destroyer of relationships and family, household, and community solidarity. However, as the converts remain connected to former surroundings, it is critical that the communicators provide the needed social and spiritual support for their newfound faith to be established. This is important so as to avoid the possibility of them reverting to their former religion and way of life under social pressure. However, the effectiveness of the communication of the gospel among the Burmese people will depend on the extent to which the prevalent separating conversion pattern is replaced by a contextual conversion pattern. One of the most critical issues for the development of a Christian communication paradigm is to establish as the goal of all mission activities the contextual conversion of the Burmese people. A contextual conversion is a genuine conversion where the converts receive a new identity as followers of Jesus, but where they are not converted out of the Burmese people context. It is a conversion where the converts remain in close contact with their own people, but instead of taking on the culture of the non-Burmese Christians, they express their new faith in Burmese cultural forms. All mission approaches and methods should be tested against this criterion of contextual conversion.

Evaluating the whole process of communication of the gospel helps determine how truly indigenous a church or contextual congregation is. Note especially its identity with the people group and its level of the full expression of Christ and the gospel to its own society. Are adequate "functional substitutes" being employed for those crucial areas of culture that would leave voids apart from relevant application from the Bible? Does the church movement have indigenous missions reaching out to other people groups? The bottom line should be judged on the basis of three **R's**: Does it have the *respect* of the Buddhist community? Is it taking *responsibility* under the Lord for ministry to the society around? Is it exhibiting *resourcefulness* in evangelizing its Buddhist neighbors and in coping with opposition from without? This study shows that there is no indigenous Burmese Christian congregation in Yangon or even in the whole country. The main reason is that the vast majority of Christian leaders still favor the traditional approach of integrating Burmese converts in the existing non-Burmese congregations. Without the establishment of Burmese congregations, communication of the gospel to Burmese people will very likely never be successful. The goal should be to establish small Burmese house fellowships, which will help Burmese converts stay within their Burmese community and culture, and which will be more effective in attracting Burmese Buddhists to the gospel. The establishment of Burmese local congregations cannot be postponed. Congregations should begin with the few converts present. All mission initiatives should be evaluated on the basis of how they contribute to the development of such contextual or indigenous congregations.

Focusing on the whole family or group is a wise and Biblical approach. Using the natural bridges of relationships, we should permeate the whole extended family or group with the gospel. Burmese Buddhist people are linked together by extended families. A network approach aimed at web movements is absolutely essential.

This study shows there is lack of cooperation between churches. Without interdenominational cooperation between churches in Yangon it will be more difficult for a further development of mission strategies, as the missiological resources of each church are limited. As pointed out mission cannot be understood without communication and communication is based on relationship. Every church leader needs to remember the fact that he is charged to take his duty of participation in the task of mission. As a piece of wood cannot burn alone, sustainable cooperation between God's people is what we need; to be aware of our missionary obligation, to plead with others, to join hands in our mission enterprises.

This study shows that the Bible plays an important role in the conversion of the Burmese people, in particular in the conversion phase and the incorporation phase. All the churches emphasized the authority and the use of the Bible in their ministry. This emphasis may be a major reason the converts exhibited strong convictions about the Bible and also key issues in the Christian faith. When the message is being related to the significant aspects of the Burmese religious and social context, a Bible-based approach helps to ensure that the message communicated remains in accordance with the biblical revelation and does not become a mere reflection of the concerns of the context.

Each Christian is a most valuable agent of the gospel for church planting and extension. They are in daily contact with the society where they work and live. Church leaders must stimulate lay movements and encourage lay teams to serve both in evangelizing the community and in nurturing new believers. Laypersons provide a rich pool of gifts, abilities, resources, personnel and energy needed to keep the momentum of the Christ-ward movement going. Home disciple groups, evangelistic Bible studies, community friendship groups, and voluntary association projects are essential for ongoing evangelization and church planting.

The Burmese people need to encounter the church because the church mediates the presence of Christ in the world and because a Christian conversion involves becoming a member of the body of Christ, which is the church, the community of God's redeemed people. In the survey it was discovered that the experience of fellowship in the church was one of the most influential factors drawing Burmese Buddhists to Christ. It was also the actual participation in worship services in church buildings where the non-Burmese Christians gathered that sparked the persecution of the seekers. Alternative approaches, therefore, have to be developed—approaches where the church comes to the Burmese people in the midst of their context and in their contextual forms.

When small Burmese house fellowships are established, they will be important places for Burmese seekers to experience Christian fellowship as a necessary preparation for their decision to become Christians. Until there are such Burmese house fellowships, the church may come to Burmese seekers where they live in the form of individual Christians, employees, and volunteers, both Burmese and non-Burmese people. On a limited scale, these Christians may offer the Burmese seekers opportunities to experience Christian fellowship, including prayers and preaching. If the persecution and social dislocation of the Burmese seekers and converts are to be reduced, it seems to be necessary to by-pass the local church buildings in which Christians from the non-Burmese ethnic groups gather and worship. This approach may not eliminate the persecution, but it will at least postpone it until a time when the seeker/convert is more mature and more ready to handle it. Furthermore, this approach will naturally lead to the establishment of Burmese house churches without any detour into the existing non-Burmese congregations.

In order to translate the goal of contextual Burmese congregations into actual Burmese house fellowships, the churches need to develop a realistic and practical procedure for church planting. The initiative for the establishment of Burmese house fellowships must come from the Christian workers employed in missional activities in cooperation with those local Christians who are most directly involved in the conversion of the Burmese people. A house fellowship may start with as few as two or three Christians, for example, one or two Burmese converts together with a mature Christian. Questions about when, where, and how often the house fellowship should gather will have to be considered, just as will questions about a liturgy. The goal, however, should be to train one of the Burmese converts to become the leader of the fellowship as soon as possible.

The Burmese converts are all around the Yangon city; therefore Burmese house fellowships initially may remain small and may be located a little distance from each other. Therefore, the churches will have to develop a system to help these house fellowships keep in contact so that they can support each other and occasionally enjoy fellowship together. In order to honor the unity of all believers in the body of Christ, the Burmese house fellowships also need to maintain their relationship with the neighboring non-Burmese local congregations. An important expression of this unity in the body of Christ is that the stronger member (the established non-Burmese congregations) helps to support and protect the weaker members (the small Burmese house fellowships). The mature local Christian who helped to establish the Burmese house fellowship can serve as the link for the house fellowship to the local congregation.

Recommendations for Further Study

Throughout this study, many issues have been mentioned without detailed analysis. While they are important to Christian communication in a Burmese Buddhist context, these issues need further research. A number of suggestions and questions for further study have emerged. Here are the most pertinent:

More research is needed in respect to the socio-cultural and religious values of Burmese people in the urban context to prove scientifically that the process of effective Christian communication is definitely changing urban Buddhists. How it affects their receptivity to the church is to be further investigated.

Related to the above is the need for research on the urban Buddhist worldviews. It would give a perspective on urban Buddhists that would help in developing better ways of communication for the Myanmar churches.

The Burmese high- and middle-classes have to be studied in much more detail. How to motivate the churches to take this segment of Burmese society seriously is a crucial question. Most current Christians are geared toward reaching the lower Burmese Buddhist class. More research on understanding middle and higher classes is needed.

Conclusion

In fulfilling the Great Commission of Jesus Christ, one of the most challenging tasks for Christians in Myanmar is how to communicate Christ in life and action intelligibly to their Buddhist neighbors. Making sense of Christ to fellow Buddhists would inevitably include preaching the gospel in their own *Dhammic* terms and faith-expressions, and relating his teachings to their thoughts and life experiences. Communicating Christ must consist of not mere verbal communication but it must involve real life situations. It is encouraging that church and mission leaders and mission partners have expressed their commitment to do mission among the Burmese people all over the country. The gospel of Jesus Christ has been presented to the Burmese people particularly in Yangon through Protestant Christians for almost 200 years. However, until now churches and mission organizations have primarily followed traditional mission principles and approaches in trying to reach the Burmese people. Consequently, today the estimated Burmese membership of Christian churches in Yangon, both Catholic and Protestant, still forms a tiny minority. The churches appear to be oblivious of two critical concerns. First, there appears to be a general lack of awareness of the missiological lessons that should be learned from the efforts of missionaries to this city in the past. Secondly, and perhaps more critically, there appears to be a general lack of interest among the communicators of the gospel in the socio-cultural and religious history of the people in this city through which God has been speaking to make himself known for centuries.

I have built on the existing theories of communication with regard to Burmese Buddhists and added new dimensions covering contextual conversion and contextual congregations within their frame of reference without losing contact with the community. Based on the findings, I developed a paradigm of Christian communication of the gospel for the Burmese Buddhists, in Yangon in particular, which states that communication is always contextual and so is its process which covers three dimensions: contextual missiological strategies, relevant Christological message and authentic ecclesiological structure with six alternative models of contextual congregation.

As a conclusion to this study, I have drawn recommendations concerning ten critical issues that must be part of a contextual model of ministry among the Burmese people in the country and Yangon in particular. The basic principles of aiming toward a contextual conversion and the establishment of contextual Burmese congregations were developed. And then, I have expanded these principles and approaches which seem to be essential elements to a paradigm for the contextual communication of the gospel. All these critical issues must be communicated to the church leaders and mission organizations, mission partners inside and outside of the country, and volunteers in missional activities in Yangon, so that they may realize the need to review the present Christian missiological weaknesses.

If the communication of the gospel to the Burmese people in Yangon is to become effective, the church leaders and mission leaders, mission partners and volunteers must be empowered to follow a more contextual model of mission. This requires that both the decision makers and the practitioners in the churches and mission organizations are taught the basic principles of this contextual model of Burmese mission through consultations and seminars. Only with the full understanding of the church and mission leadership can new approaches become effective. Finally, the mission partners must be equipped to communicate the gospel according to these contextual principles through more extensive training programs. If the communication of the gospel to the Burmese people succeeds, we will see many Burmese people from different social classes taking refuge in Jesus as the Liberator and compassionate Savior, the Word of God as their *Dhamma* and church as the *Sangha* of Christ. We will see flocks of Burmese worshiping him in their own language and expressing their new faith in their own cultural forms. At the end they will be saying *Sadu*, *Sadu*, and *Sadu*.

Bibliography

Adeney, Miriam. 2008. "Feeding Giraffes, Counting Cows, and Missing True Learners: The Challenge of Buddhist Oral Communicators." In Paul H. De Neui (ed). *Communicating Christ Through Story and Song: Orality in Buddhist Context.* PA: William Carey Library.

Allen, Roland. 1984. *The Spontaneous Expansion of the Church and the Causes Which Hinder It.* Grand Rapids: Eerdmans.

Alter, Robert. 1981. *The Art of Biblical Narratives.* New York: Basic Books.

Ariyadasa, Edwin. 2005. "Social Communication in Buddhism." In *Journal of the Asian Research Center for Religion and Social Communication* 3/2 (2005). 57-73.

Arn, Win and Charles Arn. 1982. *The Master's Plan for Making Disciples: How every Christian can be an effective witness through an enabling church.* Pasadena: Church Growth Press.

Ashin, Thittila. 2000. *Essential Themes of Buddhist Lectures.* Yangon: Department of Religious Affairs.

Baal, J. Van and Van Beek. 1985. *Symbolic Communication.* Van Gorcum: Assen.

Babbie, Earl. 2004. *The Practice of Social Research* (10th Ed). Chennai: Thomson Wadsworth.

Bailey, Stephen. 2003. "Communication Strategies for Christian Witness Among the Lao." In David S. Lim and Steve Spaulding (eds). *Sharing Jesus Christ in the Buddhist World.* Pasadena: William Carey Library.

Bosch, David J. 1993. "Reflections on Biblical Models of Mission." In James M. Phillips and Robert T. Coote (eds). *Toward the 21st Century in Christian Mission.* Grand Rapids: Eerdmans.

_____. 1982. *Transforming Mission: Paradigm Shift in Theology of Mission.* Maryknoll: Orbis Books.

Botha, P. J. J. 1992. "Letter Writing and Oral Communication in Antiquity: Suggested Implications for the Interpretation of Paul's Letter to the Galatians." In *Scriptura* 42: 17-34.

Brown, Russell E. 1968. *Doing the Gospel in South-East Asia.* Valley Forge: Judson Press.

Bunge, Frederica M. 1983. *Burma: A Country Study.* Washington DC: Government Printing Office.

Burney, C. F. 1925. *The Poetry of Our Lord.* London: Oxford.

Buttrick, David. 2008. "The Language of Jesus." In *Theology Today* 64: 423-443.

Cady, F. John. 1966. *Thailand, Burma, Laos and Cambodia.* Englewood Cliffs: Prentice-Hall.

Carey, J. W. 1975. "Mass Communication Research." In *Cultural Studies: An American View.* 1-23.

Cartlidge, David R. 1990. "Combien d'unites avez-vous de trios a quatre?; What Do We Mean by Intertextuality in Early Church Studies?" In David J. Lull (ed). *SBLASP.* Atlanta: Scholars.

Chanthavongsouk, Inta. 1999. "Buddha's Prophecy of Messiah." La Mirada, CA: The Lao Conference of Churches, 1999.

Christian Media. 2005. "Yangon Christian Directory." Yangon: Christian Media.

Cing, M. H. L. 2001. "The Place of Burmese Values in Christian Education." In *ATA Journal* 9/1 (Jan-Jun): 86-93.

Clasper, Paul. 1968. "Burma the Church amid the Pagoda." In G.H. Anderson (ed). *Christ and Crisis in Southeast Asia.* New York: Friendship Press.

Coward, Harold. 1988. *Sacred Word and Sacred Text: Scripture in World Religions.* Maryknoll: Orbis Books.

Davis, John R. 1993. *Poles Apart: Contextualizing the Gospel in Asia.* Bangalore: Theological Book Trust.

Dewey, Joanna. 1994. "Textuality in an Oral Culture: A Survey of the Pauline Traditions." In *SEMEIA* 65: 37-61.

Dhammananda, K. Sri. 2002. *What Buddhists Believe.* Kuala Lumpur, Malaysia: Buddhist Missionary Society.

Dingrin, La Seng. 2006. "A Literary Study of Adoniram Judson's Tracts with Respect to the Mutual Relationship Between Christian and Buddhist Terminology." In Festschrift Committee (eds.). *Our Theological Journey: Writings in Honor of Dr. Anna May Say Pa.* Yangon: Myanmar Institute of Theology.

Dodd, Carley H. 1982. *Dynamics of Intercultural Communication.* Dubuque: Brown.

Ebner, Eliezer. 1956. *Elementary Education in Israel in the Tannaitic Period.* New York: Block.

En, S. Kham Pau. 2003. "Key Notes Address." In Ngun Ling, Samuel, Than Win and Peter Joseph (eds). *Called to be a Community: Myanmar's in Search of New Pedagogies of Encounter*. Yangon: ATEM.

Filbeck, David. 1985. *Social Context and Proclamation: A Socio-Cognitive Study in Proclaiming the Gospel Cross-Culturally*. Pasadena: William Carey Library.

Gerhardsson, Briger. 1961. *Memory and Manuscript: Oral and Written Transmission in Rabbinic Judaism and Early Christianity*. Uppsala: Almqvistand Wiksells.

Gilliand, Dean S. 1989. *The Word Among Us: Contextualizing Theology for Mission Today*. London: Word Publishing.

_____. 1998. *Pauline Theology & Mission Practice*. Eugene, OR: Wipf and Stock.

Gittins, Anthony J. 1989. *Gifts and Strangers: Meeting the Challenge of Inculturation*. New Jersey: Paulist Press.

Gurevitch, J. Curran and J. Woolacott (eds). 1977. *Mass Communication and Society*. London: Edward Arnold.

Hall, D. G. E. *Burma*. 1998. London: Hutchinson's University Library.

Han, Thein Aung. 2003. *Myanmar Naingian Thamaing Thit 1752-1948*. Yangon: Sarpe Mwai Hlaw Thu.

Haviland, W. A. 1993. *Cultural Anthropology* (7th Ed). New York: Holt, Rinehart and Winston.

Hesselgrave, David J. 1978. *Communicating Christ Cross-Culturally*. Grand Rapids: Academic Books.

Hiebert, Paul G. 1985. *Anthropological Insights for Missionaries*. Grand Rapids: Baker Book House.

_____. 1994. *Anthropological Reflections on Missiological Issues*. Grand Rapids: Baker Book House.

_____. 1997. "Conversion and Worldview Transformation." In *International Journal of Frontier Missions* 14/2 (April- June): 84-86.

Howard, Randolph L. 1931. *Baptists in Burma*. Philadelphia: The Judson Press.

Hrangkhuma, F. 1995. "Mission as Communication." In Mattam, Joseph and Sebastian Kim (eds). *Dimensions of Mission in India*. Bombay: St Pauls.

Htay, Han and Chit Tin. 2002. *How to Live as A Good Buddhist Vol. 1*. Yangon: Department for the Promotion and Propagation of the Sasana.

Htin Aung, Maung. 1959. *Folk Elements in Burmese Buddhism*. New York: International Publications.

_____. 1967. *A History of Burma*. New York: Columbia University Press.

Indapanno, Bhikkhu Buddhadasa. 1967. *Christianity and Buddhism*. Bangkok: Sinclair Thompson Memorial Lectures.

Jenson, Ron and Jim Stevens. 1981. *Dynamics of Church Growth*. Grand Rapids: Baker House.

Jeremias, Joachim. 1969. *Jerusalem in the Time of Jesus*. Philadelphia: Fortress Press.

Jewell, Dawn Herzog. 2006. "Winning the Oral Majority." In *Christianity Today* 50/3 (March): 56-58.

Jha, Makhan. 2003. *An Introduction to Social Anthropology* (2nd Ed). New Delhi: Vikas Publishing House Private Ltd.

John, S. K. Ng. 1993. "Evangelism as Evangelizing: A Communication Perspective." In Mark L.Y. Chan (ed). *Mercy, Community, & Ministry*. Singapore: Catalyst Books.

Jones, Dale. 2008. "Moving Towards Oral Communication of the Gospel: Experiences from Cambodia." In Paul De Neui (ed). *Communicating Christ Through Story and Song*.

Kasdorf, Hans. 1980. *Christian Conversion in Context*. Scottdale, PA: Herald Press.

Kaung, Thaw. 2002. "Studies on the Ethnic Groups of Myanmar." In *Myanmar Perspective* VII/3: 26-29.

Keihl, Erich H. 1990. "Why Jesus Spoke in Parables," in *Concordia Journal* (July): 245-256.

Kelber, Werner H. 1983. *The Oral and the Written Gospel: The Hermeneutics of Speaking and Writing in the Synoptic Tradition, Mark, Paul, and Q*. Philadelphia, PA: Fortress Press.

Kennedy, George A. 1984. *New Testament Interpretation through Rhetorical Criticism*. Chapel Hill, NC: University of North California Press.

King, Winston L. 1964. *A Thousand Lives Away: Buddhism in Contemporary Burma*. Oxford: Bruno Classier.

Klem, Herbert V. 1978. "The Bible as Oral Literature in Oral Societies." In *International Review of Mission* 67/268: 479-484.

_____. 1982. *Oral Communication of the Scripture: Insights form African Oral Art*. Pasadena: William Carey Library.

Kraft, Charles H. 1974. "Distinctive Religious Barriers to Outside Penetration," In C. Richard Shumaker (ed). *Media in Islamic Culture*. Marseille, France: International Broadcasters and Evangelical Literature Overseas.

_____. 1979. *Christianity in Culture: A Study in Dynamic Biblical Theologizing in Cross-cultural Perspective*. Maryknoll: Orbis Books.

_____. 1991. *Communication Theory for Christian Witness* (rev.). Maryknoll: Orbis Books.

_____. 1991. "What Kind of Encounter Do We Need in Our Christian Witness." In *Evangelical Missions Quarterly 27 (2)*: 258-265.

_____. 2001. *Culture, Communication and Christianity: A Selection of Writings by Charles H. Kraft*. Pasadena: William Carey Library.

_____. 2008. *Worldview for Christian Witness*: Pasadena: William Carey Library.

Lat, Zau. 2006. "Reading the Great Commission." In Festschrit Committee of Myanmar Institute of Theology (eds). *Our Theological Journey*.

Leary, Catherine. 1986. "Parables and Fairytales. In *Religious Education 81/3 (Summer):* 481-497.

Legrand, Lucien. 2003. "Communication and the Bible." In *Indian Theological Studies* 40/1: 9-27.

Lim, David S. 2010. "Catalyzing Insider Movements in Buddhist Context." In Paul De Neui (ed). *Family and Faith in Asia: The Missional Impact of Social Networks*. Pasadena: William Carey Library.

Litteral, Robert L. 1988. *Community Partnership in Communications for Ministry*. Wheaton: The Billy Graham Center.

Lubeigt, Guy. 2004. "Myanmar: A Country Modelled by Buddhist Tradition." In Myanmar Historical Committee (eds). *Traditions of Knowledge in Southeast Asia Part II*. Yangon: University Press.

Mang, Aung. 2007. "Training to Effectively Communicate the Gospel in a Multi-Cultural Society." In Manfred Waldemar Kohl & A. N. Lal Senanayake (eds). *Educating for Tomorrow: Theological Leadership for the Asian Context*. Bangalore: SAIACS Press.

Manuel, A. D. 1994. *Communication and the Church*. New Delhi: ISPCK.

Maung Tin, Pe. 1961. "Presenting the Gospel of Christ within the Given Culture and Its Context." In *Southeast Asia Journal of Theology* 3/2 (October): 20-28.

McGavan, Donald A. 1955. *The Bridges of God: A Study in the Study of Missions*. New York: Friendship Press.

_____. 1970. *Understanding Church Growth*. Grand Rapids: Eerdmans.

_____. 1992. "A Church in Every People: Plain Talk about a Difficult Subject." In Ralph D. Winter and Steve C. *Perspectives on the World Christian Movement: A Reader*. Pasadena: William Carey Library.

Ministry of Education, 2004. "Development of Education in Myanmar." Yangon: Ministry of Education.

Myaing, Htun. 1991. *Myanmar Culture*. Yangon: Ministry of Information.

Myanmar Council of Churches. 2002. *Collections of Professor U Khin Maung Din's Papers & Articles*. Yangon: MCC.

Naing, Ko Ko. 1997. *Studies in the Dhamma of Buddha for Seminaries in Myanmar*. Yangon: MICT.

Nash, M. 1965. *The Golden Road to Modernity: Village Life in Contemporary Burma*. London: John Wiley and Sons.

Nawl, Cung. 2004. "Why Myanmar Church Fails in Evangelizing the Buddhist Bamar People in Myanmar." Yangon: [n.p].

Ngun Ling, Samuel. 2001. "Doing Theology Under the Bo Tree: Communicating the Christian Gospel in the Bama Buddhist Context" in *Rays: MIT Journal of Theology* 2 (January): 73-84.

_____. 2006. "Communicating Christ Cross-Culturally: A Dialogical Approach to Mission and Theology in 21st Century Myanmar." In MIT Festschrift Committee (eds). *Our Theology Journey*. 33-51.

_____. 2007. "A Burmese Christian's Responses to Social Values of Work, Consumption, and Economic Options in Myanmar." In *Myanmar Journey of Theology* 5 (March): 68-74.

_____. 2007. "Voices of Minority Ethnic Christians in Myanmar." In *CTC Bulletin* (June): 1-6 accessed on 6/6/08.

Nida, Eugene A. 1960. *Message and Mission*. Pasadena: William Carey Library.

Niles, D. T. 1968. *Who Is This Jesus?* Nashville: Abingdon Press, 1968.

Nyo, Kyaa. 2000. Maung. *Presenting Myanmar*. Yangon: Today Publishing House.

Nyunt, Kan. 1999. *Myat Buddha Myat Nibban and Dana, Thila, Bwana*. Yangon: Ein Gyin Nyunt Sarpay.

Nyunt, Khin Maung. 2005. *Myanmar Traditional Monthly Festivals*. Yangon: Innwa Book Store.

Nyunt, Moe Moe. 2008. "Burmese Reactions to Christianity." In *Ray: MIT Journal of Theology* 9 (January): 104-122.

Palakeel, Joseph. 2007. *The Bible and the Technologies of the Word*. Bangalore: Asian Trading Corporation.

Parshall, Phil. 1984. *New Paths in Muslim Evangelism: Evangelical Approaches to Contextualization*. Grand Rapids: Baker Book House.

Pe, Hla. 1985. *Burma: Literature, Historiography, Scholarship, Language, Life and Buddhism*. Singapore: Institute of South East Asian Studies.

Pentecost, Edward C. 1982. *Issues in Missiology: An Introduction*. Grand Rapids: Baker Book House.

Perry, Peter. 2007. *Myanmar (Burma) since 1962: The Failure of Development.* Aldershot, UK, Ashgate.

Purser, William C. B. *1931. Christian Missions in Burma.* Westminster, England: Society for Propagation of the Gospel in Foreign Parts.

Rubin, Herbert J and Irene S. Rubin. 1973. "Effects of Institutional Change upon a Dependency Culture: The Commune Council 275 in Rural Thailand." In *Asian Survey* 13/39: 269- 278.

Sanneh, Lamin. 1989. *Translating the Message: The Missionary Impact on Culture.* Maryknoll: Orbis Books.

Sayadaw, Webu. 1997. "The Essence of Buddha Dhamma." [n.p].

Seamands, John T. 2000. *Tell It Well: Communicating the Gospel Across Cultures.* Chennai: Mission Educational Books.

Shaw, R. Daniel and Charles Van Engen. 2003. *Communicating God's Word in a Complex World: God's Truth or Hocus Pocus?* New York: Rowman & Littlefield Publishers.

Sjoberg, Gideon. 1960. *The Preindustrial City: Past and Present.* New York: Free Press.

Smalley, William A. 1992. "Cultural Implications of an Indigenous Church." In Ralph D. Winter and Steve C (eds). *Perspectives on the World Christian Movement.*

Smith, Alex G. 2008. "Communication and Continuity through Oral Transmission." In Paul H. De Neui (ed). *Communicating Christ Through Story and Song.*

Smith, Donald Eugene. 1965. *Religions and Politics in Burma.* Princeton, NJ: Princeton University Press.

Smith, Donald K. 1992. *Creative Understanding: A Handbook for Christian Communication Across Cultural Landscapes.* Grand Rapids: Zondervan.

Soe, Tin. 2005. "An Economic Interpretation of Some Myanmar Tradition Concepts in the Context Globalization." In Myanmar Historical Commission (eds). *Traditions of Knowledge in Southeast Part III.* Yangon: University Press.

Sogaard, Viggo. 1993. *Media In Church and Mission: Communicating the Gospel.* Pasadena: William Carey Library.

_____. 1996. *Research In Church and Mission.* Pasadena: William Carey Library.

Spiro, Melford E. 1970. *Buddhism and Society: A Great Tradition and Its Burmese Vicissitudes* (2nd ed.). Berkeley: University of California Press.

Stott, John R. W. 1975. *Christian Mission in the Modern World.* London: Falcon.

Stults, D. L. 1989. *Developing An Asian Evangelical Theology*. Manila: OMF Literature.

Sundersingh, Julian. 2001. *Audio-Based Translation: Communicating Biblical to Non-Literate People*. Bangalore: SAIACS Press.

Syrjanen, Seppo. 1987. *In Search of Meaning and Identity: Conversion to Christianity in Pakistani Muslim Culture*. Vammala, Finland: Missiologian Ja Ekumeniikan Seura R.Y.

Taber, Charles R. 1978. "Is There More Than One Way to Do Theology?" In *Gospel in Context* 1/1:143-154.

Taylor, Robert B. 1973. *Introduction to Cultural Anthropology*. Boston: Allyn and Bacon Inc.

Thwin, M. Aung. 1985. *Pagan: The Origins of Modern Burma*. Honolulu: University of Hawaii Press.

Tippett, Alan R. 1977. "Conversion as a Dynamic Process in Christian Mission." In *Missiology: An International Review* 5/2 (April): 203-221.

Trager, Helen G. 1966. *Burma Through Alien Eyes: Missionaries Views of the Burmese in the Nineteenth Century*. Bombay: Asia Publishing House.

Tun, Than. 1988. *Essays on the History and Buddhism of Burma*. Scotland: Kiscadale Publications.

_____. 2004. *Studies in Myanmar History Number One*. Yangon: Inwa Books.

Van Engen, Charles E. 1981. *The Growth of the True Church: An Analysis of the Ecclesiology of Church Growth Theory*. Amsterdam, Netherlands: Rodopi.

_____. 1996. *Mission on the Way: Issues in Mission Theology*. Grand Rapids: Baker Books House.

Van Rheenen, Gailyn.1996. *Missions: Biblical Foundations & Contemporary Strategies*. Grand Rapids: Zondervan.

Vincentius, Sangermamo. 1833. *A Description of the Burmese Empire*. London: Susil Gupta.

Vuta, K. T. "A Brief History of Planting and Growth of the Church in Burma." D.Miss, Dissertation, Fuller Theological Seminary, 1983.

Wa, Maung Shwe. 1963. *Burma Baptist Chronicle*s. Rangoon: Burma Baptist Convention.

Walls, Andrew F. 1996. *The Missionary Movement in Christian History: Studies in the Transmission of Faith*. Maryknoll: Orbis Books.

Wayland, Francis. 1853. *A Memoir of the Life and Labors of the Rev. Adoniram Judson Vol.2*. Boston: Sampson and Company.

Wilson, Carl. 1976. *With Christ in the School of Disciple Building: A Study of Christ's Method of Building Disciples.* Grand Rapids: Zondervan.

Win, Kambawza. 1988. "Colonialism, Nationalism and Christianity in Burma." In *Asia Journal of Theology* 2/2: 270-281.

Win, Kyaw, Mya Han and Thein Hlaing. 1991. *Myanmar Politics 1958-1962.* Yangon: Universities Press.

Yangon Development Committee. 1999. *Yangon: Green City of Grace.* Yangon: The Yangon City Development Committee.

Yaw, Pa. 2006. "Christian Conversion: an Evaluation on Judson's Mission Approach." In MIT Festschrift Committee (eds). *Our Theology Journey.*

Yoe, M. Shway. 1963. *The Burman: His Life and Notions.* New York: The Norton Library.

Yeo, Peggy. 1993. "The Family as a Community of Mercy and Ministry." In Mark L. Y. Chan (ed). *Mercy, Community, & Ministry.*

APPENDIX A

Demographic Questionnaire for Interviewees

Code _____

Age_____

Years of full-time ministry _____

Denominational Affiliation_____

Leadership Category: Local Pastor, Denominational/Organizational Leader, Bible School Teacher

APPENDIX B

Interview Questions

In order to collect contemporary information about communicating the gospel to Burmese Buddhists, the interviews were conducted with twenty Christian leaders from different Protestant churches in Yangon. The analysis of the data led to suggestions for communicating the gospel message effectively to this group. The operational questions fall into four categories.
1. General Principles
2. Methods
3. Barriers
4. Acceptance

As an outworking of the basic operational questions (OQ), the following sub-questions (SQ) were used to guide the development of specific interview questions.

OQ.1. General Principles
   A. In your opinion, what are the characteristics of a good communicator of the gospel to Burmese Buddhists?
   B. What does gospel communication mean to you?

OQ.2. Methods
   A. What specific methods do you currently use to communicate the gospel to Burmese Buddhists? Please give specific examples.
   B. Why do you use these methods?
   C. In communicating the gospel, how do you make it easily understood by the Burmese Buddhists?

OQ.3. Barriers
   A. If you are finding that the majority of Burmese Buddhists are not responsive to the gospel, what might be the reasons? Please be specific.
   B. What limitations do you face in communicating the gospel to Burmese Buddhists?
   C. What kinds of barriers do you believe Burmese Buddhists have to face before deciding to accept the gospel? Please give specific reasons.

OQ.4. Acceptance
   A. Do you think any Burmese Buddhists to whom you have communicated the gospel, will respond to the gospel? Could you give specific results, please?
   B. If you find some Burmese Buddhists accept the gospel, what might be the contributive factors? Please be specific?

APPENDIX C

Questionnaire for the Burmese Buddhist Converts in Yangon

This questionnaire is being used for the purpose of personal research. You don't need to write your name or address on the questionnaire, as it is anonymous. Please tick your chosen answer that you feel is most correct. There is no right or wrong answer. Your answer is correct if it expresses your true opinion.

1. What is your gender?
    a. Male
    b. Female
2. How old are you now?
    a. Under 20
    b. 20 to 29
    c. 30 to 39
    d. 40 to 49
    e. 50+ . . .
3. What is your marital status?
    a. Single
    b. Married
4. What is your education level?
    a. Primary School
    b. Middle School

c. High School
   d. College/University
   e. Other (Specify---)
5. What is your occupation?
   a. Christian Minister
   b. Government Servant
   c. Company Employee
   d. Unemployed
   e. Other (Specify---)
6. How long have you been in Yangon?
   a. 1-3 years
   b. 4-6 years
   c. 7-10 years
   d. 11-15 years
   e. Born in Yangon
7. How many years ago did you first become interested in becoming a believer in Jesus Christ?
   a. 1 to 3 years ago
   b. 4 to 7 years ago
   c. 8 to 10 years ago
   d. 11+ years ago
8. How many years ago were you baptized?
   a. Last year
   b. Two years ago
   c. Three to seven years ago
   d. Eight+ years ago

Questionnaire for the Burmese Buddhist Converts in Yangon

Please indicate for each of the persons or methods listed below how much they helped you to become aware of the gospel (before conversion), to decide to become a Christian (at conversion), and to be taken care of as a new convert (after conversion).

To what extent, were any of the following people involved in your conversion to Christianity?			Not Really (1)	Some (2)	Much (3)
9.	Professional Christian Minister	Before Conversion			
10.		At Conversion			
11.		After Conversion			
12.	Lay Person (Burmese Buddhist Convert)	Before Conversion			
13.		At Conversion			
14.		After Conversion			
15.	Family Member	Before Conversion			
16.		At Conversion			
17.		After Conversion			
18.	Friend or acquaintance	Before Conversion			
19.		At Conversion			
20.		After Conversion			

Did any of the following contribute to your conversion?			Not Really (1)	Some (2)	Much (3)
21.	Radio	Before Conversion			
22.		At Conversion			
23.		After Conversion			
24.	Jesus Film/Movie	Before Conversion			
25.		At Conversion			
26.		After Conversion			
27.	Audio Cassettes	Before Conversion			
28.		At Conversion			
29.		After Conversion			
30.	Bible or portions of the Bible in Burmese	Before Conversion			
31.		At Conversion			
32.		After Conversion			
33.	Tripitaka-Certain passages	Before Conversion			
34.		At Conversion			
35.		After Conversion			
36.	Books or tracts in Burmese	Before Conversion			
37.		At Conversion			
38.		After Conversion			
39.	Bible Study Group	Before Conversion			
40.		At Conversion			
41.		After Conversion			
42.	Bible Correspondence Course	Before Conversion			
43.		At Conversion			
44.		After Conversion			

Questionnaire for the Burmese Buddhist Converts in Yangon

Did any of the following contribute to your conversion?			Not Really (1)	Some (2)	Much (3)
45.	Educational Program (Health Education, Tailoring, Handicraft, Teaching English or Computer)	Before Conversion			
46.		At Conversion			
47.		After Conversion			
48.	Community Service (micro-enterprise, medical treatment)	Before Conversion			
49.		At Conversion			
50.		After Conversion			
51.	Intercession by Christians	Before Conversion			
52.		At Conversion			
53.		After Conversion			
54.	Prayer with Christians	Before Conversion			
55.		At Conversion			
56.		After Conversion			
57.	Personal witness by one or more people group	Before Conversion			
58.		At Conversion			
59.		After Conversion			
60.	Dialogue between Christians and Buddhists	Before Conversion			
61.		At Conversion			
62.		After Conversion			

Were there certain experiences which influenced you towards faith in Christ?			Not Really (1)	Some (2)	Much (3)
63.	Observing the lifestyle of a particular Christian or group of Christians	Before Conversion			
64.		At Conversion			
65.		After Conversion			
66.	Miracles or observing the power of Christ in a specific situation	Before Conversion			
67.		At Conversion			
68.		After Conversion			
69.	Answered Prayer	Before Conversion			
70.		At Conversion			
71.		After Conversion			

Did any Christian beliefs, teachings or practices make it difficult for you to become a Christian or to remain a Christian?			Not Really (1)	Some (2)	Much (3)
72.	The Christian Doctrine of the Trinity	Before Conversion			
73.		At Conversion			
74.		After Conversion			
75.	Crucifixion of Jesus Christ	Before Conversion			
76.		At Conversion			
77.		After Conversion			
78.	The Way Christians worship God (e.g. usage of drums, language)	Before Conversion			
79.		At Conversion			
80.		After Conversion			

Questionnaire for the Burmese Buddhist Converts in Yangon

Were there social or political influences which made it difficult for you to become a Christian or remain Christian?		Not Really (1)	Some (2)	Much (3)
81.	Pressure from Buddhist family members	Before Conversion			
82.		At Conversion			
83.		After Conversion			
84.	Pressure from Buddhist community	Before Conversion			
85.		At Conversion			
86.		After Conversion			
87.	Pressure from Buddhist Religious Leaders	Before Conversion			
88.		At Conversion			
89.		After Conversion			
90.	Not welcome by Christian churches	Before Conversion			
91.		At Conversion			
92.		After Conversion			

Did you have any of the following ideas about Christianity which made it difficult to become or to remain a Christian?		Not Really (1)	Some (2)	Much (3)
93.	Christianity is a Western religion	Before Conversion			
94.		At Conversion			
95.		After Conversion			
96.	Christianity is not a religion for Burmese	Before Conversion			
97.		At Conversion			
98.		After Conversion			
99.	Christians have a secular lifestyle, low morality, etc.	Before Conversion			
100.		At Conversion			
101.		After Conversion			

To your knowledge, do you regard any of the following factors as important to your conversion or experience as a Christian?			Not Really (1)	Some (2)	Much (3)
102.	There was a Christian church in this area	Before Conversion			
103.		At Conversion			
104.		After Conversion			
105.	Worship form made me feel comfortable	Before Conversion			
106.		At Conversion			
107.		After Conversion			
108.	Other Christians made me feel welcome in their fellowship	Before Conversion			
109.		At Conversion			
110.		After Conversion			

Langham Literature and its imprints are a ministry of Langham Partnership.

Langham Partnership is a global fellowship working in pursuit of the vision God entrusted to its founder John Stott –

> *to facilitate the growth of the church in maturity and Christ-likeness through raising the standards of biblical preaching and teaching.*

Our vision is to see churches equipped for mission and growing to maturity in Christ through the ministry of pastors and leaders who believe, teach and live by the Word of God.

Our mission is to strengthen the ministry of the Word of God through:
- nurturing national movements for training in biblical preaching
- multiplying the creation and distribution of evangelical literature
- strengthening the theological training of pastors and leaders by qualified evangelical teachers

Our ministry

Langham Preaching partners with national leaders to nurture indigenous biblical preaching movements for pastors and lay preachers all around the world. With the support of a team of trainers from many countries, a multi-level programme of seminars provides practical training, and is followed by a programme for training local facilitators. Local preachers' groups and national and regional networks ensure continuity and ongoing development, seeking to build vigorous movements committed to Bible exposition.

Langham Literature provides majority world pastors, scholars and seminary libraries with evangelical books and electronic resources through grants, discounts and distribution. The programme also fosters the creation of indigenous evangelical books for pastors in many languages, through training workshops for writers and editors, sponsored writing, translation, strengthening local evangelical publishing houses, and investment in major regional literature projects, such as one volume Bible commentaries like *The Africa Bible Commentary*.

Langham Scholars provides financial support for evangelical doctoral students from the majority world so that, when they return home, they may train pastors and other Christian leaders with sound, biblical and theological teaching. This programme equips those who equip others. Langham Scholars also works in partnership with majority world seminaries in strengthening evangelical theological education. A growing number of Langham Scholars study in high quality doctoral programmes in the majority world itself. As well as teaching the next generation of pastors, graduated Langham Scholars exercise significant influence through their writing and leadership.

To learn more about Langham Partnership and the work we do visit **langham.org**

www.ingramcontent.com/pod-product-compliance
Lightning Source LLC
Chambersburg PA
CBHW071225170426
43191CB00033B/1665